Microsoft Flight Simulator 2024 for Professionals

Mastering Realistic Flight Dynamics, Weather Systems, and Advanced Navigation

TABLE OF CONTENT

CHAPTER 1

INTRODUCTION TO MSFS 2024

Microsoft Flight Simulator has been the benchmark for flight simulation for more than 20 years, connecting both professional pilots and aviation enthusiasts to the thrill of flight with every new release. The latest Microsoft Flight Simulator 2024 follows suit, delivering one of the most significant updates in the series' history. With more powerful planes, stunning visuals, and improved third-party support, this next-gen simulator has got it all. Here's everything you need to know—complete with new plane features and room-scale VR support—so you can soar into the next gen with complete assurance.

The History of Microsoft Flight Simulator

Microsoft Flight Simulator has been wowing gamers with its superb realism, flying over world landmarks, and witnessing live weather. One of the largest and most popular sim franchises, it never stopped trying to advance the immersion level. In 2024, it even surpasses that with high-end aircraft simulations, more accurate controls, and visuals that will make virtual flight as realistic as possible.

The home will be entering the markets on the 19th of November, so from business and military aircraft to intensified environmental effects and controls, buckle up for an air travel experience like no other.

Thrilling Breakthroughs from the Developer Livestream

During a live stream by developers some time back in late April, Microsoft showcased pages of new aircraft highlighting their focus on realism and diversity like the Amphibian Aerospace Albatross, the Airbus family A330, A321LR, A350, and the Beluga XL.

Through collaborations with developers like iniBuilds and contributions from real-life pilots, every single plane is pre-loaded with super accurate cockpits and very realistic flight dynamics. This contributes immensely to players' ability to simulate various types of flight-from passenger civilian planes all the way up to military transport missions.

FOCUS ON NEW AIRCRAFT

Amphibian Aerospace Albatross: Flight Versatility

One of those remarkable additions is the Amphibian Aerospace Albatross, one very rare aircraft that can take off and land on water as well as on land. It is a quite versatile plane since it provides flights over vacant lakes or Oceanic oceans. It provides an adventurous and flexible experience for adventurous pilots.

The Airbus Collection: A330, A321LR, and A350

With its inclusion of work along with iniBuilds, MSFS2024 is bringing highly detailed recreations of Airbus: the A330, Extended Range A321, and A350. These aircraft were carefully carried from conceptual design to cockpits being configured out into flight aerophysics because they will actually occur under natural conditions. A330 & A350: This helps far-off travelers in offering extensive touch for their realistic aeroplanes; pilots will certainly go further in flying extensive distances.

A321LR: An adaptable choice for shorter route lengths, providing a taste of new Airbus efficiency to the player.

Military Aviation: The A400M Atlas

The A400M Atlas is perfect for military aviation enthusiasts. With a really rugged construction, the A400M is favorite among military flyers for its immense cargo-carrying capacity globally. For simmers who want to challenge themselves, attempting to fly it through adverse weather with heavy payloads raises the simulation challenge bar much higher.

The Cargo Giant: Beluga XL

Arguably the most visually stunning of all the planes in the line-up, Beluga XL has been designed to carry oversized freight-like sections of aircraft. With its strange whale-like shape, this plane brings a whole new logistical puzzle to the game, allowing players to manage huge cargo loads instead of passengers.

Next-Level Graphics and Realistic Environments

Microsoft Flight Simulator 2024 keeps pushing the boundaries of realism with several advanced rendering methods being implemented. Dynamic weather conditions like accurate lighting and realistic terrain will make every flight-over the Alps or inserted into a storm-entirely realistic with fresh graphics engines.

Actual rain, thunderstorms, and even mist add another level of depth to the realism element. The pilots must adapt through shifting conditions since every flight is unique.

The Best Flight Simulation Hardware for Maximum Immersion

Microsoft Flight Simulator 2024 is optimized to use a variety of peripherals, giving the player an immersive experience through realistic control and VR support. Some of the best hardware available to take your flight simulation to the next level includes:

Pimax VR Headsets: Total Immersion

For the most realistic experience, Pimax VR headsets have ultra-high field of view and high-definition displays. The headsets place gamers in the cockpit, with great spatial awareness and a feeling that flight is actually occurring.

Turtle Beach: High-Precision Flight Controllers

Turtle Beach provides PC and Xbox-compatible flight yokes, throttles, and pedals. The controllers feel like the resistance and sensitivity of real aircraft controls, giving gamers a realistic piloting experience.

Tobii Eye and Head Tracking: Seamless Navigation

The Tobii eye and head tracking technology revolutionizes cockpit interaction by allowing pilots to control their view with simple head movements. This intuitive feature increases situational awareness and reduces the necessity for manual camera control.

Elgato Control Panels: Streamlined Operations

Elgato's control panels that can be adjusted make cockpit control easier, with the most critical functions assigned to physical buttons. For game players in intricate flights, this could be beneficial in fluidly navigating and communicating.

Thrustmaster Flight Controls: Precise for Enthusiasts

As for the joysticks and rudder pedals, no one provides more realism than Thrustmaster. The wildly fine-tuned controls provide the accuracy at precisely those very crucial moments of takeoff or landing, and it is precisely why serious flight simmers love them.

What to Expect on Launch Day

With the release date of November 19 approaching closer and closer, excitement is in the air. Microsoft has been busy with numerous promotions on social media to create hype, especially on its new Threads account, where it gives updates, tips, and behind-the-scenes details. Users of the simulator are also looking forward to the release, with high hopes from new aircraft, additions, and updates on the environment.

Part of the Microsoft Flight Simulator Community on Threads

For Microsoft, this journey has been the means of engaging with fans who love flight simulation, learning from one another, and keeping up to date. Threads will enable enthusiasts to network with fellow enthusiasts face-to-face at events and be up-to-date about the best ways to leverage the potential in Microsoft Flight Simulator 2024.

Conclusion: Setting the Standard for a Flight Simulator

Microsoft Flight Simulator 2024 is one step further in the progression of flight simulation, breaking into new realms of realism, diversity of planes, and depth. For the seasoned pilot or newbie fresh off the runway, this iteration will redefine the extent to which players can experience virtual flight. With breathtaking graphics, extensive selection of aircraft, and state-of-the-art peripherals, prepare to experience an adventure like no other among the clouds.

OVERVIEW OF THE MSFS 2024 VERSION

Microsoft Flight Simulator 2024 has finally landed, and big thanks to Xbox Game Studios for letting us review it.

Given all those years of radio silence during 2006 to 2020, Flight Simulator is presently on a well-established release timetable. Until you get close enough, Microsoft Flight Simulator 2024 appears to have very little to offer short of what the company put out in 2020-the-40th Anniversary Edition, so to speak if you want. Look closer, however, and you will find a whole heap of new items which are relatively interesting, at least if more than just pilots flying aeroplanes is to your liking.

Let's go through the main distinctions between Microsoft Flight Simulator 2024 and its 2020 predecessor. At first glance, the two do feel reasonably similar, since Xbox didn't really go out of their way to present differences.

One of the largest additions is the new career mode, which adds surprising depth to the game. Players begin by mastering the basics of flying—take-offs, landings, taxiing, and obeying Air Traffic Control commands—before sitting for an exam to receive their private pilot's license. From there, advancement is dependent on finishing missions based on your current license level, making money to pay for your next exam, and working your way up to larger and more sophisticated planes.

That makes this mode even more immersive: the option to begin at any airport or airfield in the world. Missions are then customized to your location, providing some genuine sense of purpose. Unlike its 2020 iteration, where flying was less goal-oriented, this structured format provides players with clear objectives and a reason to continue improving.

Microsoft Flight Simulator 2024 takes the amazing tech presented by the 2020 model and expands the entire world out with satellite information. It then calculates this data into landscapes, buildings, trees, and even meticulously hand-modeled landmarks and cities through photogrammetry. This realism makes it one of the highest-definition models of the Earth on any video game-you can even fly over your house and recognize it.

The graphics are equally as breathtaking, provided your computer is capable of high-quality settings. Other than flight, you are able to step out of your plane to carry out pre-flight inspections or merely appreciate the airplane up close, and all these have been well recreated.

Hard-core simmers will welcome that Microsoft Flight Simulator 2024 is so realistic. Switch off the assists, and it's a stern test: voice communications from ATC, takeoff and landing, dealing with the weather as it comes, real-time style, and piloting your way through busy skies. Yes, if you need to unwind, there's free flight mode to let you cruise around the skies with all helps switched on and stress-free flight.

For a more structured exam of your abilities, the game also includes scenarios: short missions in which you fulfill particular tasks and try to earn leaderboard ranks-everything from performing a challenging landing to racing against other people in an effort to create the fastest time.

It's not all perfect, though—and I'm not just talking about the real-time weather. One of the game's weaker points is its reliance on AI-generated voices.

While AI is appropriate for managing ATC communications worldwide—it allows the game to take advantage of infinite airfields, towns, and cities without employing hundreds of pre-recorded voice lines—some of the AI voices just aren't that great.

AI for air traffic control, neat-but does my flight instructor also have to be AI? Or the passenger I'm giving a sightseeing tour of Leeds to? Unlikely. While the ATC and radio dialogue are nice, anything other than that radio filter sounds a little too robotic. For a game trying to achieve this level of immersion, realistic world, a poorly executed voice line can momentarily yank you out of the game.

Microsoft Flight Simulator 2024 does have some more significant changes over the predecessor. It has twice as many planes from the base game, 70 in total, and also 150 meticulously hand-crafted airports. A career mode and scenarios add a little more to doing than the simple free-flying sandbox it was. Little things like visual grime on planes accumulating and just overall more diversity on the landscape bring it in as far as immersion goes.

As such, Microsoft Flight Simulator 2024 is a good upgrade if you're a frequent flight sim user and require the best and latest. The caveat: being online-only, it streams a huge amount of data in real-time. In my general experience, connectivity problems were few and far between, but that's not to say the occasional get-kicked-off mid-flight wasn't maddening.

Steam Deck Performance

This is one of the earliest subpar Steam Deck and Linux titles. It was playable after a while when Proton was updated to enhance compatibility even more. On November 29th, 2024 you ought to be able to play the game with Proton Experimental [Bleeding Edge] with some fixes.

Adding `DXVK_HDR=0 %command%` as a launch parameter if gaming on a Steam Deck OLED might be required, as it may allow you to bypass loading problems.

Recommended Settings for 30 FPS

To keep performance level at 30 FPS stable on SteamOS, a 30 FPS frame cap should be activated with the TDP cap turned off. The game defaults to the "low-end" preset but can be tweaked further. Deflate settings like terrain shadows, foliage, and other environmental factors down to Low. Then, switch the upscaling mode to FSR 2 and set it to Performance mode.

Tweaking these settings, we're getting around 26-30 FPS while flying over Central Park in New York City—one of the most demanding areas in the game. In less crowded regions, like rural landscapes and small towns, the frame rate climbs above 30 FPS. However, this performance is based on flying a small propeller plane.

The most it suffers from is the plane type you choose: huge planes suffer to reach 30 FPS, and even flying huge planes over congested cities-particularly around massive airports like JFK-can make the plane crash nonstop. This is where unless you're comfortable flying small aircraft, the game is not particularly playable.

Performance & Battery Life

Steam Deck pulls constantly high power, always 21-22W and never 20W. Thus LCD owners are receiving at most approximately 1.5 hours of battery life, while OLED owners are receiving somewhat more than 2 hours.

During game playing, CPU and GPU temperatures come to rest around 70°C.

Accessibility Features

As one would expect from a first-party Microsoft game, Microsoft Flight Simulator 2024 hits the gate running with accessibility features. The game has speech-to-text and text-to-speech for in-game chat so voice users and text chat users can communicate with each other. There is even auto-translate for text chat during cross-lingual play.

The following list of customizations that are available:

- Camera shake toggle: on/off
- Control remapping ability

It can be modded to feature:

having font size control; mine's at 22 for readability

- HUD opacity increased for better presentation of text
- screen narrator used for menu navigation
- subtitles for in-game communication between aircraft and Air Traffic Control

Microsoft Flight Simulator 2024 introduces a career mode, additional planes, and a couple of additional scenarios to the fold. Whether or not these justify the cost of a whole new game depends on how much you enjoy the series. If free-flight exploration is your main interest, the 2020 game still plays well.

Impresses on the Steam Deck are great, first flying wee craft-trainers, usually manages performance above 25 FPS on single-prop planes, fighter aircraft, or private jets. It is jetliners, however, that simply can't maintain more than 15-20 FPS with constant crashes that make the game practically unplayable. Maybe Proton updates and further optimizations by Asobo will remedy this, but I would not buy Microsoft Flight Simulator 2024 on the Steam Deck right now.

WHAT MAKES IT DIFFERENT FROM PREVIOUS RELEASES

Release Date & New Features

Microsoft Flight Simulator 2024 releases on November 19, both in the PC and Xbox versions, trying to establish the benchmark for next-generation simulation experiences that aficionados around the globe yearn for. Fresh aircraft is showcased throughout, ranging from low-flying small planes cut out for bush flying to behemoth brutes for business air travel.

Game Editions & Pricing

Microsoft has released four digital versions that will likely appeal to various appetites, but for those who want something tangible to be included in this experience, there is also a Collector's Edition.

And here they are:

- Standard - £69.99
- Deluxe - £99.99
- Premium Deluxe - £129.99
- Aviator - £199.99

All of the versions feature some number of aircraft and improved airports. Microsoft explained that they did not create new handcrafted airports but improved airports from 2020. Scroll For More

Standard Edition (70 Aircraft, 150 Airports)

The Standard Edition reaches new players or casual flyers with 70 aircraft, 30 of which are new additions such as the Airbus A321LR, Boeing 737 MAX 8, and A-10 Thunderbolt II. 40 base planes from MSFS 2020 have been upgraded with new avionics, flight systems, and features.

New aircraft highlights:

- Airbus A330 (-200, -300, 300P2F)
- Airbus A330-743L Beluga XL
- De Havilland DHC-6 Twin Otter
- Fairchild Republic A-10 Thunderbolt II
- Robinson R66

This edition appeals to those gamers primarily interested in the explorer and free-flying role more than building their aircraft collection.

Deluxe Edition 75 Aircraft, 155 Airports

The Deluxe Edition extends the base of the Standard Edition by adding 5 more aircraft + 5 upgraded airports (based on the base of the 2020 simulator).

Exclusive planes featured in this edition:

- Cessna 188 AGTruck
- Cessna 404 Titan
- Cessna 408 SkyCourier
- Dornier Seastar
- Amphibian Aerospace G111/HU16

Good choice for those who like to fly in general aviation (GA) airplanes and want a bit more flexibility without going to the Premium Deluxe level.

Premium Deluxe Version (95 planes, 160 airports)

Whereas the Premium Deluxe Edition is reserved for players requiring a higher assortment and comes with 95 airplanes-10 additional than in the Deluxe version-and 5 enhanced airports.

Exclusive aircraft in this edition:

- Boeing C-17 Globemaster III
- Boeing 747-400 Global Supertanker
- Boeing 747-400 LCE Dreamlifter
- Boeing CH-47D Chinook
- Saab 340B
- Pilatus PC-24

This edition also comes with a "Jumbo Steelbook" physical release that contains a pilot lanyard and ID badge holder and will thus be a collector's delight.

Aviator Edition (Ultimate Collection)

The Aviator Edition is the biggest of the trio, accompanied by 30 additional Microsoft-exclusive planes to make it the ultimate edition for hardcore flight sim enthusiasts who must have everything.

It will come in a number of different editions for the serious and casual simmers, with varying aircraft to test out Microsoft Flight Simulator 2024. The Standard Edition will suffice for the beginners, while the Premium Deluxe and Aviator editions will offer more choices for those who want a longer flying experience.

Microsoft Flight Simulator 2024 – Collector's Edition

For hardcore flight sim enthusiasts, the Collector's Edition is the definitive simulation experience that combines the Aviator Edition with a set of extremely collectible physical items. This edition is extremely low-print run.

WHAT'S IN THE BOX?

Find seven exclusive one-of-a-kind items that elevate your Microsoft Flight Simulator experience:

- **Antonov AN-225 Model (1/400 scale) with Stand** - A collectible scale model of the legendary airplane.
- **Flight Bag & 6-Patch Set** - Aviator-inspired bag with embroidered patches.
- **Collectible Retail Box -** Nice-looking box for display.
- **Logo Pin** - Metal logo pin with official MSFS logo.
- **Flight Tags/Keychain with Variable Game Code** — Exclusive keychain with a variable game code.
- **Collectible Lithograph** — Limited print commemorative to the game.
- **Letter to Fans** — Handwritten letter from the development team.

Pre-Order Details

Preorders for any version of Microsoft Flight Simulator 2024 will be available up until November 18th, prior to the official launch date of November 19th.

To find out more on what is planned with MSFS 2024, watch FSNews.

SYSTEM REQUIREMENTS AND INSTALLATION

Since its release in November 2024, Microsoft Flight Simulator 2024 has set a new gold standard for flight simulation, with graphics and features that surpass those of any other simulator. Whether you're a seasoned virtual pilot or just starting to take your first flights, the right hardware configuration is the key to enjoying the most out of this next-generation simulator.

Here in this book, we talk about the various system requirements comparing different hardware configurations that will allow one to understand what it takes to have an optimal flight experience.

Overview of System Requirements

Component	Min Spec (NVIDIA/Intel)	Recommended Spec (NVIDIA/Intel)	Ideal Spec (NVIDIA/Intel)
CPU	Intel Core i7-6800K	Intel Core i7-10700K	Intel i7-14700K
GPU	GeForce GTX 970	GeForce RTX 2080	GeForce RTX 4080
RAM	16 GB	32 GB	64 GB
VRAM	4 GB	8 GB	12 GB
Storage	50 GB	50 GB	50 GB
Bandwidth	10 Mbps	50 Mbps	100 Mbps

To really get the most out of Microsoft Flight Simulator 2024 (MSFS 2024), proper hardware is needed. Whether it's the absolute minimum to play or a powerhouse setup, you can make wise upgrade decisions based on the system requirements.

System Requirements Overview

- Operating System: Windows 10 (minimum)
- DirectX Version: DirectX 12 (DX12) required

Below is a summary of the specifications taken directly from Microsoft's official Flight Simulator 2024 FAQ. Price estimates to upgrade hardware can vary based on market conditions and model availability.

Understanding the Hardware Requirements for Flight Simulator 2024

Minimum Specifications

This is the baseline needed to run MSFS 2024. While you'll be able to load and play the game, expect lower frame rates, reduced graphics quality, and possible performance drops in demanding scenarios like dense cities or extreme weather conditions.

Recommended Specifications

For a smoother and more immersive experience, aim for the recommended specs. This ensures better graphics, stable frame rates, and a more enjoyable flight experience across various environments.

Ideal Specifications

If you want the ultimate MSFS 2024 experience, the ideal specs will allow you to crank up the settings, run the game at high resolutions, and maintain smooth performance—even with multi-monitor setups, VR, or demanding aircraft add-ons.

KEY HARDWARE PARTS DETAILED

CPU (Processor)

The CPU is the brain of MSFS 2024 and does real-time weather, physics, and massive world data calculations. The less stuttering gameplay, the better the CPU performs, especially in challenging flight scenarios.

GPU (Graphics Card)

The GPU is responsible for rendering the game's stunning graphics. And the more powerful the GPU, the better the textures, the higher the resolutions, and the smoother the frame rates—especially when flying over detailed scenery or in challenging weather conditions.

CPU vs. GPU: How They Work Together

Think of your rig as a restaurant:

The CPU is the executive chef, managing orders, directing everything, and making the key decisions.

The GPU is the kitchen personnel, taking the chef's orders to prepare the final meals.

If the chef (CPU) is slow, the kitchen (GPU) won't be able to serve meals efficiently. And if the kitchen personnel (GPU) are weak, even the best possible chef (CPU) cannot set things in motion properly. A good balance between CPU and GPU is the key to maximum performance.

RAM (Memory)

More RAM helps MSFS 2024 deal with huge volumes of real-time data more gracefully, especially with add-ons installed or when flying in dense environments.

Storage (SSD vs. HDD)

Though the game size remains the same in any setup, an SSD reduces loading times by a huge margin and improves scenery streaming performance.

Internet Bandwidth

Since MSFS 2024 streams in real-time world and weather data, a stable and quick internet connection allows for better visual fidelity and current world rendering.

Upgrading Your System for MSFS 2024

Upgrade Priorities:

✅ CPU & GPU: Provide the biggest performance impact.

✅ If at minimum specs: Upgrade to at least recommended specs for noticeable performance improvement.

✅ Future-proofing: Invest in hardware higher than the suggested specs if budget allows.

✅ Don't forget peripherals: A nice yoke, joystick, or throttle can make your flying so much more enjoyable.

MSFS 2024 Release Details

Microsoft Flight Simulator 2024 launched on November 19, 2024, and is available on:

✔ PC

✔ Xbox Series X & S

✔ Xbox Cloud Gaming

If you set it up properly, then you can really enjoy the stunning realism of MSFS 2024. 🛫

THE RIGHT PC FOR MICROSOFT FLIGHT SIMULATOR 2024

Microsoft Flight Simulator 2024 comes out on November 19, and will be one of, if not the most, system-intensive game ever created. Most people will be playing it on a computer that meets minimum or recommended specs, but playing it on max settings takes seriously heavy hardware to accomplish.

Here at Chillblast, we are experts in high-end gaming PCs. Whether a state-of-the-art 4K gaming system with ray tracing or extremely budget-friendly but smooth-as-butter 1080p gaming, we will be able to provide you with a customized PC within your budget.

Let's take a look at the system requirements for MSFS 2024 and figure out which of the following is best suited to provide this next-gen flight experience:

Component	Minimum requirements	Recommended requirements	Ideal requirements
CPU	AMD Ryzen 5 2600X or Intel Core i7-6800K	AMD Ryzen 7 2700X or Intel Core i7-10700K	AMD Ryzen 9 7900X or Intel Core i7-14700K
Graphics	AMD Radeon RX 5700 or NVIDIA GeForce GTX 970	AMD Radeon RX 5700XT or NVIDIA GeForce RTX 2080	AMD Radeon RX 7900XT or NVIDIA GeForce RTX 4080
RAM	16GB	32GB	64GB
VRAM	4GB	8GB	12GB
Storage	50GB	50GB	50GB
Bandwidth	10Mbps	50 Mbps	100 Mbps
Operating System	Windows 10 with the latest update	Windows 10 with the latest update	Windows 10 with the latest update

Minimum System Requirements for Microsoft Flight Simulator 2024 – What You Need to Know

Well, honestly, operating Microsoft Flight Simulator 2024 isn't exactly the domain of cutting-edge hardware-most modern gaming computers will run the program with no problems.

Basic Hardware Requirements

- Processor: AMD Ryzen 5 2600X or Intel Core i7-6800K (or better)
- Memory: 16GB RAM
- Graphics Card: AMD Radeon RX 5700 or NVIDIA GeForce GTX 970 (or better)
- VRAM: 4GB
- Storage: 50GB
- Internet Speed: 10 Mbps

- Operating System: Windows 10 (latest update)

WHAT THIS TRANSLATES TO FOR YOUR PC

Keep in mind that listed processors are relatively ancient mid-range processors, so the majority of gaming esktops manufactured last couple years won't be an issue and neither will a lot of laptops. And 16GB of RAM has been the sweet gaming standard for years.

For graphics cards, the recommended models—Radeon RX 5700 and GTX 970—are relatively reasonable, and as of recent Steam hardware surveys, more than half of PC gamers already own a card at or above this tier.

Internet Connection is Important

As opposed to most single-player games, Microsoft Flight Simulator 2024 requires an internet connection to work, even for core features such as real-time weather information or cloud computing. Thankfully, 10 Mbps is relatively low-moderate bandwidth, and most homes, especially in the UK, are running higher than that.

Windows 10 Support & Future Considerations

Even though Windows 10 is the recommended version, pay attention to the fact that Microsoft will discontinue official support, including security patches, in October 2025. So, if you are yet to upgrade from Windows 10, you can think of shifting to Windows 11 soon.

What Performance Can You Expect?

If your machine has all of the following, then Microsoft's guesstimate is that you'll be able to play the game at 1080p resolution at 70% scaling with all of the settings set to low and still hold about 30 frames per second. This will not be the most enjoyable sight, but at least you'll be able to play it.

If your current PC does not meet Microsoft Flight Simulator 2024's system specification requirements, or you are a complete newbie to gaming hardware, then Chillblast can assist. With several years' experience of working with high-spec game PCs, we have designed MSFS-specific PCs that are seriously powerful at very competitive prices.

Best Budget PC for MSFS 2024: The Jetson Ryzen 5 RTX 4060

The Jetson Ryzen 5 RTX 4060 is a great option for those looking to get into MSFS 2024 without breaking the bank. At this price, it will easily surpass the minimum requirements and enable you to play the game at silky smooth frame rates without needing to turn down your settings.

Key Features:

✅ **Processor** – AMD Ryzen 5 7600 (6 cores, 12 threads, high clock speed) for cool and efficient performance

✅ **Graphics** – NVIDIA GeForce RTX 4060 8GB VRAM with full support for NVIDIA DLSS upscaling

✅ **Memory** – 16GB DDR5 RAM for gameplay and responsiveness

✅ **Storage** – 1TB SSD for quick loading and enough space

✅ **Connectivity** – Built-in Wi-Fi and Gigabit Ethernet

✅ **Case** – DeepCool CH370, a thin and nicely designed mid-tower case

With this setup, you'll enjoy smooth 1080p gameplay with impressive visuals and stable frame rates—all at an affordable price.

Recommended System Requirements for MSFS 2024

To play the game on high settings at 1440p, the following hardware is recommended by Microsoft:

- CPU: AMD Ryzen 7 2700X or Intel Core i7-10700K or similar
- RAM: 32GB
- GPU: AMD Radeon RX 5700XT or NVIDIA GeForce RTX 2080 or similar
- VRAM: 8GB
- Storage: 50GB SSD
- Internet Speed: 50 Mbps
- OS: Windows 10 latest update

These are pricey parts for the era, but much less expensive alternatives exist today. The 8-core CPU requirement is just a bit noteworthy, since flight sims are really CPU-intensive, so an even faster six-core processor may not be enough.

If you need to add additional RAM, it's one of the easiest DIY upgrades that you can perform. Just be sure that you get the right speed and generation for your system.

The other issue to consider is the internet bandwidth. It needs 50 Mbps to be able to get real-time weather and landscape update. In case you have numerous devices in your network, you may incur lag; thus, make sure that the connection can handle the load.

Microsoft estimates 1440p resolution, high detail, and approximately 30 FPS with the above specifications.

Best Prebuilt PC for MSFS 2024: The Albatross Core i5 RTX 4070 SUPER

For more frame rates and 1440p gaming, the Albatross Core i5 RTX 4070 SUPER can be your powerful, future-proofed buddy.

Highlights:

Processor – Intel Core i5-14500(14 cores, 20 threads) - One of the powerful processors when it comes to multi-threaded performance;

- ✅ **Graphics** — NVIDIA GeForce RTX 4070 SUPER with 12GB of VRAM for the next-generation graphics and performance;

- ✅ **Memory** — 32GB DDR5 RAM for rapid data processing;

- ✅ **Storage** — 1TB SSD for incredibly fast loading;

- ✅ **Advanced Features** — Enables NVIDIA DLSS and frame generation to obtain enhanced frame rates.

The RTX 4070 SUPER outperforms even the last-gen flagship, the RTX 3090, for a steal. With this 12GB VRAM, this build remains up-to-date with the needs of today and will most definitely be future-proofed for any future updates in any flight sim.

You can play Microsoft Flight Simulator 2024 at 1440p with high frame rates on this computer and reap the full rewards of NVIDIA's AI-based performance boosts for a seamless experience.

Whether you're new to PC gaming or building a performance machine to fly away with flight sims, let Chillblast build a custom PC to your exact requirements. Option for the Jetson Ryzen 5 RTX 4060 for buttery-smooth 1080p play or the Albatross Core i5 RTX 4070 SUPER for a seriously powerful 1440p with frame rates to match.

Ideal System Requirements for Microsoft Flight Simulator 2024 – The Ultimate Experience

If you'd like to get Microsoft Flight Simulator 2024 up to its limit, Microsoft has included an "Ideal" list of system requirements for 4K resolution, Ultra-settings, and 40-50 FPS frame rates—with future improvements making that increasingly likely for 60 FPS.

Ideal Hardware Specs

- Processor: AMD Ryzen 9 7900X or Intel Core i7-14700K (or better)
- Memory: 64GB RAM
- Graphics Card: AMD Radeon RX 7900XT or NVIDIA GeForce RTX 4080 (or better)
- VRAM: 12GB
- Storage: 50GB
- Internet Speed: 100 Mbps
- Operating System: Windows 10 latest update

What These Specs implies

4K Ultra support for any game is not easy, but Microsoft Flight Simulator 2024 takes it to the extreme. Some of the quickest CPUs out there are enumerated below, only bested by a select few ultra-high-end options.

But then maybe the surprise here is in the 64GB RAM requirement, possibly a first for a flagship game to have put to paper such a high bar. Putting that into perspective, Microsoft then released a statement to clarify that it wouldn't be necessarily used all at once, but reserving such a huge amount of RAM ensures that a minimum of 32GB is always committed to Flight Sim, with the rest keeping background apps in check.

On the graphics front, both Radeon RX 7900XT and RTX 4080 are top-of-the-line GPUs-short of the best. If you haven't upgraded your PC recently, it will be a stretch to get this kind of performance out of current hardware.

THE BEST GAMING PC FOR MICROSOFT FLIGHT SIMULATOR 2024

If you're looking for a beastly machine that not only meets but exceeds these requirements, a high-end gaming PC like the Thunderbolt Ryzen 7 RTX 4080 SUPER is a top choice.

Why This PC Stands Out

- Powered by the AMD Ryzen 7800X3D – One of the best gaming CPUs with eight high-performance cores and extra 3D V-Cache for ultra-smooth gameplay.
- 64GB DDR5 RAM for seamless multitasking and overkill performance.
- 2TB Super-Speed SSD Storage for blistering loading into the game.
- GeForce RTX 4080 SUPER with 16GB of VRAM and new-gen CUDA cores; this GPU will run at least with ease beyond 60 FPS in Flight Simulator 2024.
- DLSS 3 & Frame Generation Support – NVIDIA's latest AI-powered tech enhances frame rates even further while keeping the stunning 4K visuals intact.

If you're aiming for the absolute best Microsoft Flight Simulator 2024 experience, these ideal system specs will deliver breathtaking visuals and smooth performance at the highest settings. But keep in mind—this level of performance requires serious hardware.

CHAPTER 2

GETTING STARTED WITH FLIGHT SIMULATION

Leaping into home flight simulation can be intimidating initially. There's equipment to choose, software to master, and getting it all to play well together—then, naturally, there's actually flying!

But don't worry—we're here to simplify the process.

If you're into flight training or just for the enjoyment of operating a flight simulator, this book will walk you through what you'll need to do to get started without spending hours and hours conducting your own research.

Getting into Flight Simulation

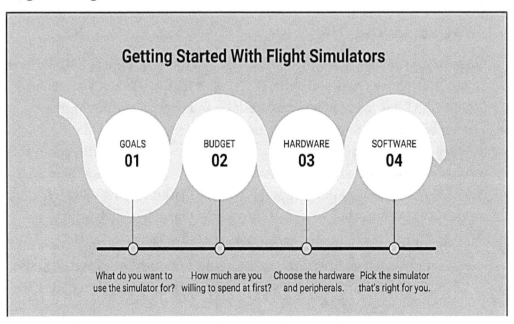

There is no single right or wrong way of starting your own flight sim because no two people's budgets, training goals, or chosen aircraft are the same. Complex setups evolve from simpler ones and it is the best suggested plan we offer you as well.

For this reason, take the following into account briefly:

☑ **Your goals** – Are you flying for recreation or to become a real-world pilot?

✅ **Your budget** – Knowing how much you're willing to spend on will help narrow down options.

Once you have those figured out, choosing the right equipment becomes a lot easier.

Core Flight Simulator Equipment

You don't need a huge setup to start, though, just a few critical pieces.

1. PC, Xbox, or Mac

Your flight simulator platform is the basis of your setup. Though there are some mobile versions, for example, iPad apps, they are not as powerful as PC, Xbox, or Mac, so we'll be focusing on those.

2. Flight Controls (Joystick / Yoke + Throttle Quadrant)

No controls partially destroy the thrill of a flight simulator.

Joysticks: Some models have built-in throttle controls.

Yoke + Throttle Quadrant: More realistic for commercial airplane simulators and more enjoyable.

3. Keyboard & Mouse

You can just get a regular wireless keyboard and mouse. These will be useful in camera controls as well as to interact with the switches in the cockpit.

4. Audio – Headset or Speakers

Good audio makes an enormous difference in immersion.

Speakers: Surround sound is great but very expensive and a pain to set up.

Headset: A $60 aviation-style headset can provide great audio quality along with a built-in microphone for online communication.

Enhancing Realism – Understanding Immersion & Value

Once you have the fundamentals, flight sim magic occurs with immersion-a feeling of presence in the cockpit.

Believe it or not, it's the small things that can make a huge amount of difference in terms of adding realism:

✅ Flying with a genuine aviation headset instead of gaming headphones

✅ Your controls being at the right height for a more realistic feel

✅ Tweaking display setup for greater immersion in the field of view

But that is where the law of diminishing returns kicks in.

Major improvements are all in the $0-5,000 range: at this point, quality controls, good visuals, and online ATC services give you good value for your money.

After that, you can add motion platforms, professional-grade panels, and custom cockpits, but the cost-benefit curve starts to flatten.

Bottom line? Start with quality fundamentals, then add immersive features most vital to you in increments.

A Glimpse Inside an Actual Flight Simulator Setup

Now that we've covered the basics, let's see how all of these components together look in a real flight simulator setup.

A fully loaded configuration incorporates all of these elements into a profoundly immersive home cockpit environment-though keep in mind, each configuration is unique!

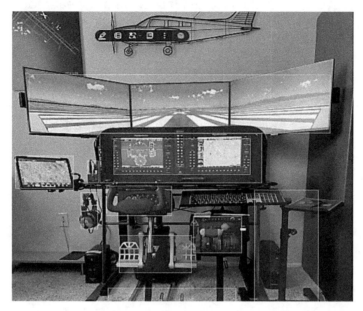

This setup boots X-Plane 12 onto an Apple Mac Studio M1 Max, providing a powerful foundation for flight simulation. An iPad ForeFlight is employed as an Electronic Flight Bag (EFB), offering real-time navigation and flight planning functions. PilotEdge handles realistic air traffic control (ATC) interactions, and Navigraph updates navigation charts for seamless and realistic flight.

INSIGHT OF A HOME FLIGHT SIMULATOR OWNER

Establishing a flight simulator involves future planning. One owner who went through some important lessons while doing so had this to say:

- Think Long-Term When Selecting a computer
- This is where the discussion ends.

Secondly, were I to have gone back in time and did it all again, I would have bought a gaming PC rather than a Mac. That stated the Mac Studio does run relatively well used in single monitor mode when I appended it on with three 4K monitors I really felt and sensed its doing its best work. This is what restricts how much further I can get by adding further complicated addons or very advanced models of aircraft.

Plan Your Setup with Future Upgrades in Mind

Don't decide what operating system you're going to use until you think about how much you want to expand your sim in the future. While Macs are great at some things, they don't offer the scalability or hardware options of PCs, especially if you need a very high-end GPU.

Monitor Mounting is Important

It was important to have a fully adjustable monitor mount. For anyone considering a Sim-Lab triple monitor system, be aware to closely consider the height requirements such that the vertical supports are tall enough for your set up.

Custom Mods Can Add in Realism

To make it even more realistic in feel, I added a Cirrus throttle mod from ProDeskSim to my Honeycomb Bravo. The new one is greatly improved; the old one was too short and this made accessing some switches terribly inconvenient.

Lighting Increases Immersion

A tiny LED light strip at the rear of the monitor, connected to power via a USB plug, provided night flying as a whole different proposition. Backlight provides a subtle realism that is otherwise missing.

I realize this is a case of an advanced setup, you don't at all have to build your simulator in this way, you can start with something very rudimentary and then add your rig bit by bit as the years go by.

How Much Does a Home Flight Simulator Cost?

It's nice to know the price range for home flight simulators before choosing your configuration.

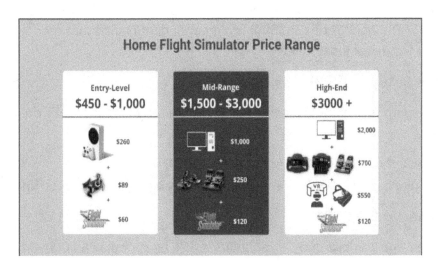

Future-Proofing: Is It Worth It?

It's easy to start with the minimum, but flight sim software keeps improving. Here's why forward planning is a good thing:

Hardware Requirements Increase: Over time – With each new MSFS or X-Plane update, hardware limits are stretched ever further. What works well now might falter tomorrow.

Add-ons Are Resource-Intensive – Weather engines, better graphics, and highly detailed aircraft take more processing power.

New Tech: VR, Photorealistic Scenery, etc. If you require assistance for VR or highly realistic landscapes, then you will require a very powerful CPU and GPU.

Spending Smart, if possible, invest in hardware one step ahead of today's need, mainly on your CPU and GPU.

Modular Upgrades – Choose a PC with a good motherboard and power supply, so you can upgrade individual components later rather than having to buy a new system.

BREAKDOWN OF HOME FLIGHT SIMULATORS

Entry-Level Setup ($450 – $1,000)

If you already have a gaming PC or Xbox, you only require:

- Microsoft Flight Simulator ($60)
- Joystick + throttle combo ($89)
- Total: $149 (assuming you already have a PC or Xbox)

- No PC? The Xbox Series S ($300) is a great budget choice that can run Microsoft Flight Simulator just as well.

Mid-Range Setup ($1,500 – $3,000)

A good setup with rudder pedals and a better computer will really make the experience come alive.

- Joystick, throttle, and rudder pedal set ($250)
- Gaming PC ($1,500+) – Runs everything but VR and max visual settings.

High-End Setup ($3,000+)

For top-of-the-line graphics and VR capability, you'll be spending $3,000–$4,000 on a powerhouse system.

Keep in mind: You don't have to buy it all at once; you can start with a lessor system and add components gradually over time.

CHOOSING THE RIGHT FLIGHT SIMULATOR SETUP

Now that you have an idea of what to expect in terms of cost, let's figure out the best configuration for you.

1. Define Your Goals

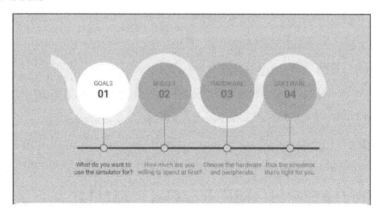

Ask yourself:

Are you flying for fun? If yes, flexibility is critical-you need to have the capability to try out various planes and conditions of flight.

Are you training to fly real? You need a setup that is as similar to the plane you fly in reality as possible.

A mix of both? Try to simulate your real aircraft but have the flexibility to fly others when needed.

2. Set a Budget

Decide how much you're comfortable spending now, knowing you can always upgrade later.

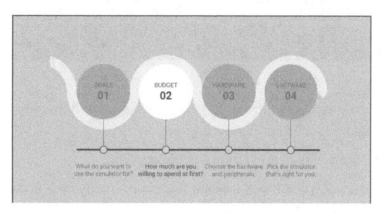

3. Select Your Hardware

You will at least require:

- A PC, Mac, or Xbox
- A TV or monitor
- A joystick, yoke, and throttle
- (Optional but highly suggested) Rudder pedals
- A headset or speakers

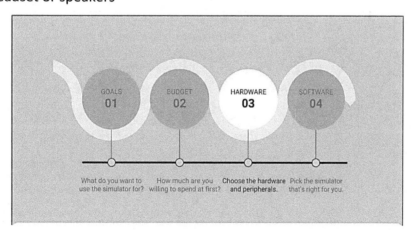

PC vs. Mac vs. Xbox: Which is Best for Flight Sim?

Platform	Pros	Cons
PC	Most powerful, expandable, supports third-party add-ons, best for VR	Expensive upfront
Xbox	Budget-friendly, smooth performance, easy to set up	Limited customization, only runs MSFS
Mac	Good for X-Plane, simple setup ↓	Limited simulator options, not upgradable

Bottom Line:

Serious simmer: Yes, remove PC from the options since it will always be upgradable to whatever is being introduced in the future.

Casual, lower budgets: Great visual from the boxes: Xbox.

For those Mac users: Yes, start with X-Plane since you already have a Mac—that would just give you greater room toward expansions down the line.

Which Flight Simulator to Choose

The best simulator depends on your needs:

- Microsoft Flight Simulator (MSFS) – Best visuals, suitable for casual and serious simmers. Can be used with PC and Xbox.
- X-Plane 12 – Real physics, suitable for serious pilots and Mac users.
- Prepar3D – Suitable for actual pilot training but requires a powerful PC.

32

WHICH FLIGHT SIMULATOR TO CHOOSE?

If you're venturing into flight simulation, you must have asked yourself: Which one is the best?

In the world of civilian flight simulators, there are two of the best that stand supreme:

- Microsoft Flight Simulator (MSFS)
- X-Plane

For those who want to fly military, the option is DCS World, with an experience like no other with combat scenarios and fighter aircraft.

There are other options, such as Prepar3D, Infinite Flight, and FlightGear, but for the common person, MSFS and X-Plane are where to start.

Microsoft Flight Simulator (MSFS) – The King of Graphics

MSFS is the best-selling flight simulator out there, and it's not hard to understand why: it has undergone some significant performance, feature, and overall reliability enhancements since its release.

WHAT SETS MSFS APART?

☑ **Breathtaking Graphics** - Plain and simple, no one does graphics like this, with high-def textures, superb lighting, and satellite imagery that will make the world come alive before your eyes. Even some places include 3D photogrammetry to make it absolute realism.

☑ **Immersive Sound**: The sound design is clean and very well-executed, further immersing you in believing that you're in the cockpit.

☑ **Strong Community & Frequent Updates**: Supported by Microsoft, MSFS has a huge user base, with frequent waves of updates that will keep this title up to date for many years to come.

Looking for a visually beautiful, immersive, and well-supported flight simulator, it's hard to ignore Microsoft Flight Simulator.

Microsoft Flight Simulator (MSFS) may be nice to gaze at, but it hasn't been trouble-free. It has had reliability and performance issues since launch. While many of these have been improved, it still falls behind X-Plane in the stability department.

Flight dynamics-wise, MSFS has made monumental strides over its predecessors. Nevertheless, X-Plane still remains the best in delivering the most realistic flight model.

The second area where MSFS has not triumphed is customization. If you want to model the aircraft you fly, be my guest and get to work on your research. Not all aircraft and avionics have been brought into MSFS but X-Plane has a lot more choices.

Why X-Plane Is Unbeatable

There is a reason why X-Plane is used so extensively in commercial flight simulators. It provides the most realistic flight experience with tremendous customization options and is one of the most stable.

If you've got a custom avionics setup in the real world-a combination-and-match panel-X-Plane lets you replicate it. But where it lags behind MSFS is in visual detail, specifically terrain rendering. If you're going to rely on visual references for navigation, X-Plane might be more challenging, but it won't affect instrument flying (IFR).

DCS World: The Military Simulation Experience

DCS World is for those pilots who want to fly high-performance military aircraft. It's a sophisticated, immersive simulator where realism is the key, and it's no surprise that many real-life pilots are players.

You can learn to fly in DCS, but generally, it's easier to get the fundamentals under your belt in MSFS or X-Plane first. Warning: DCS is possibly highly addictive!

Choosing! the Right Controls

The right flight controls can really add to your simulator experience. Here are a few things to consider:

- Yoke or Joystick? If the aircraft you fly in the real world has a yoke, get one. If it's a joystick, that's the way to go.
- Do You Fly More Than One Type of Aircraft? If you'll be flying both airplanes and helicopters, a joystick is the way to go.
- Need More Buttons? Complex and military aircraft usually have many controls, so you'll require a joystick or throttle with plenty of buttons.

GOOD FLIGHT CONTROLS TO BUY

- Honeycomb Flight Controls (Has an Xbox Compatible Version)
- Thrustmaster T.1600M FCS HOTAS
- Logitech G Flight Controls
- Thrustmaster T-Flight HOTAS One (For Xbox)
- Logitech Extreme 3D Pro

Do You Require Rudder Pedals?

Rudder pedals add a bit of realism to the simulator, especially in ground control and crosswind landings. But does it require it? Not likely.

Most joysticks have a twist or rocker feature which simulates rudder movement. Not as accurate as actual pedals, but if you're short of money or space, it'll suffice.

Flight simulators can also simulate rudder control if necessary.

If you're going to be in it for the long haul, rudder pedals are an investment to make. Otherwise, you can wait until you're ready

Recommended Rudder Pedals

- Thrustmaster Pendular Rudder
- Logitech G Pro Flight Rudder Pedals
- Thrustmaster TFRP Rudder

How to Choose the Best Monitor for Flight Simulation

You don't need an ultra-high-end monitor, but visuals are important to immersion. Here's what to consider

Resolution Problem - A 1440p or 4K display provides a clearer picture of the world, but more powerful computers are required at higher resolutions.

Refresh Rate Problem - Although 240Hz refresh or 144Hz does remove blur from imagery, flight sims are demanding, so a high refresh rate monitor will not benefit you.

Screen Sweet Spot - 32" or 27" with 4K is the sweet spot for sharpness.

How Many Monitors? - Three monitors bring it to the next level with immersion. Good alternative: one ultrawide monitor.

Suggested Monitors

- Samsung UJ59
- Samsung S50GC (Ultrawide)

Choosing a Flight Simulation Headset

A good headset will enhance your immersion and you will be able to talk on networks like VATSIM and PilotEdge.

- **Budget Choice**: HyperX Cloud II (~ $70)
- **Radio Headsets**: Movement flexibility but need battery maintenance.
- **Ultimate Options:** The surround sound sound, although the headsets tend to be the better value.

Do You Need Head Tracking or VR?

Not needed, but head tracking or VR greatly increases the realism level.

Head Tracking – Allows you to shift your head from side to side to glance about the cockpit. Especially wonderful for VFR flying and military flight sims.

VR- Fully immerses you in a 3D cockpit that gives you a depth perception feeling, but your PC will need to be powerful enough to run it properly.

Multi-Monitor setup- Immerses you and does not need head tracking and VR.

Simply begin with a single standard monitor and later upgrade as required.

If you desire an immersive experience, the addition of physical buttons, knobs, and switches takes it to the next level; configuring avianics using a mouse can soon become exasperating; hardware panels provide the real McCoy.

REALSIMGEAR

Anything from single G1000 individual panels to full Cirrus Cockpit setups in hardware.

Air Manager – is able to display custom-designed panels on extended monitors. Now, add it to a touch screen, and you have it: realistic AVIATIONS.

Knobster: Small box that allows a user to control avionics knobs in the absence of a mouse, ideal to be used by VR users.

Logitech Panels: The majority of panels which all work independently that provide functionality from radios and autopilot.

If flying is what you are interested in, these additional items will prepare your home extremely close to piloting an actual aircraft.

SETTING UP YOUR CONTROLS

First, launch Microsoft Flight Simulator 2024. This is the only way to configure your controllers since, apart from inside the simulator itself, you will be unable to do so. Launch the simulator and at the top right-hand side, a menu is where "CONTROLS" will be located.

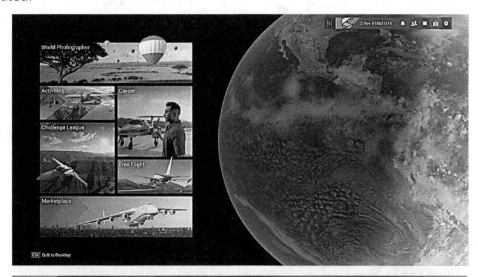

At the top left of the menu, you will see the plane you have presently selected. To change, simply click on it with your mouse. This section enables you to choose an aircraft and set up custom controller profiles for it. Further details on this are found later in the book.

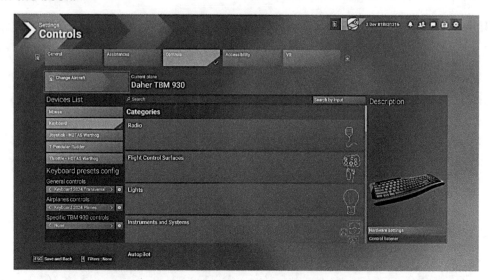

On the left side of the window, you see a list of all of the controllers currently attached to your PC and identified by the simulator. Choose the one you'd like to configure from this list prior to making changes.

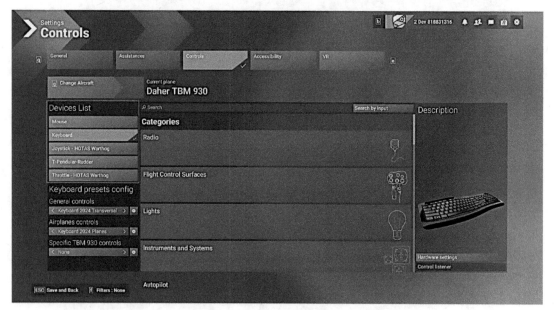

THE THREE MAIN CONTROL PRESETS

Below the list of connected controllers are three preset categories:

1. General Controls – These settings apply to all aircraft in any scenario.

2. Aircraft Category Controls: Settings can be applicable to aircraft types, for example, airplanes, rotorcraft, and gliders.

3. Aircraft Specific Controls: These are settings for the currently selected aircraft, which allow different keybinds specific to that model.

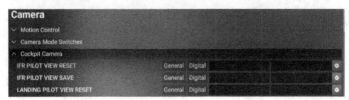

All these groups have default profiles, but you can switch between them or select a custom profile you defined by using the arrow keys of the menu. The user interface shows each command clearly, so it is easier to recognize which controls belong to which group.

Individual Aircraft Type Controls

These are specific to the model of the aircraft. For instance, if you're flying a Cessna 172, Boeing 737 Max, or a Robinson R66, whatever keybinds you set up will be particular to that model and none other. For instance, although two aircraft are from the same class-like Guimbal Cabri G2 and Airbus H125 (helicopters), each can have their own unique keyboard.

You can duplicate, rename, reset, or delete any of these profiles by clicking the gear icon next to the profile name.

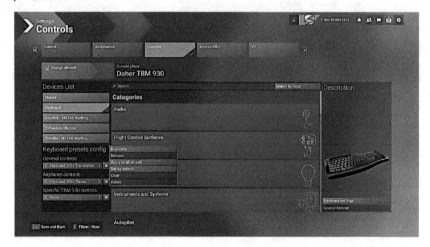

Identifying Mapping Conflicts

If any of your control mappings have conflicts, a number will appear next to the binding, as illustrated below.

To see which commands are competing, click the cog symbol next to the mapping. This displays a list showing all other functions that have been assigned to that button, key or switch.

Applying Filters

Filters option at the bottom, upon being clicked, opens a dropdown where one can toggle between the following:

- None – showing all possible bindings.
- Assigned – displaying the presently utilized ones only.
- Critical – defining solely the most critical controls.

Yes, they are useful while creating a personalized profile from the default only, since it is easy and fast to unload the unnecessary bindings at the very beginning.

Search Options

At the head of the center of the screen is a magnifying glass icon to search for commands.

Simply type "brake" or "autopilot" and it will show all its bindings. Thus, binding functions to your controller is a piece of cake.

To the right of the search bar is a box that reads "Search by input". Clicking this allows you to see if a specific button or axis of your controller has been mapped.

Simply click "Search by input" and hit the button or move the axis on your controller.

If no functions are displayed then the button/axis is not assigned to anything.

When many functions appear, this may indicate multiple mappings, which you can resolve to avoid conflict.

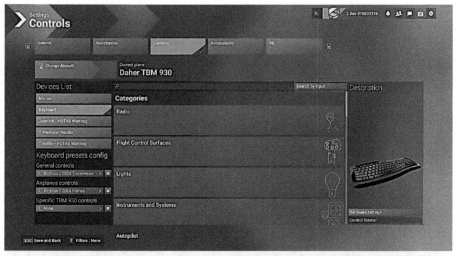

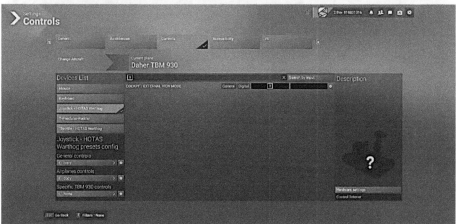

Microsoft Flight Simulator 2024 controller inputs: these are divided into categories. You can explore these categories to know their subcategories and uses, which you can assign to your controller.

If you're only viewing some categories or your partial mappings, look at your Filters setting and ensure it's set to None to show all options.

This version of the simulator offers greater control of input settings so you can remap nearly every cockpit function-what is normally done with the mouse-to your controller. So, for example, you can remap: Airbus battery switches, Fuel switches, Autopilot controls, onto your controller buttons, if it is properly recognized by the simulator.

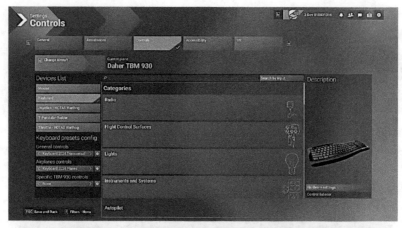

On the right side of the screen, you can view a complete description of each function that is available for mapping. Just hover your mouse over a function to view more about what it does.

Below the description box, you find the "Hardware Settings" menu. You click it to adjust the sensitivity of your controller. Be sure you choose the right controller and adjust the correct axis so that you are very precise in the settings.

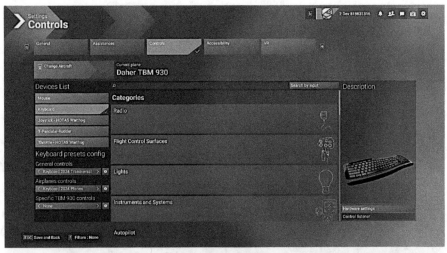

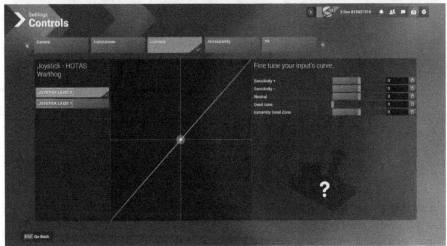

Controller Setting Changes in Flight

You can always change your control settings while playing. To do so, stop the game and then go to settings and then Controls. Or simply open the toolbar and click on the controller icon at the top-left corner to change your controls there directly.

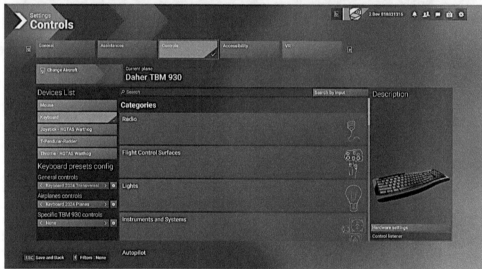

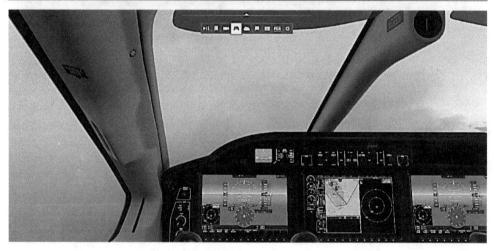

UNDERSTANDING THE MAIN MENU AND INTERFACE

Microsoft Flight Simulator 2024 settings have been grouped into five categories that can be accessed by clicking the settings wheel in the main menu:

- General
- Assistances
- Controls (For a comprehensive guide on controller settings, refer to our "Controller Settings FAQ" article.)
- Accessibility
- VR

Some of these settings are different from where they appeared in Microsoft Flight Simulator 2025. For instance, VR settings that in the earlier version were under General settings now have their own section.

General Settings Overview

The General Settings menu provides an array of features to personalize your flight experience, including how the following are configured:

- Graphics - Adjust settings that influence visual quality and performance.
- Language - Adjust your in-game language.
- Sound - Adjust audio settings for the simulator.
- Online - Configure settings for multiplayer and live weather.
- Camera - Configure camera angles and camera movement.
- Traffic – Alter AI and real traffic settings.
- Flight Model – Choose realistic or simplified flight dynamics.
- Flight Interface — Tune HUD and cockpit interaction settings.
- Advanced Options — Options like Developer Mode and other tweak settings.

Take some time to get familiar with these menus before your initial flight and establish settings for your liking.

Assistance Settings

Personalize flight assistants to your level of skill. Perhaps you'd prefer all assists off or on, or let the AI pilot take some of your flying for you. Click on the arrows on the menu bar to toggle between "Default Assists" and "All Assists", depending on your level of control.

Accessibility Settings

Tweak the game's interface for a more comfortable experience, such as:

- **Subtitle size** - Adjust the size of the font so it becomes readable.
- **Narration -** Voice guidance on/off.
- **Effects & Animations** - Change the visual effects according to your need.

VR Settings

Adjust VR-specific settings like graphics and traffic to create that simulated flight experience. They are only in effect when using VR mode and with the headset inserted.

To switch between 2D mode and VR mode, navigate to the "VR Mode" menu and select "Switch to VR", or utilize the shortcut CTRL+TAB.

CHAPTER 3

NAVIGATING THE WORLD IN MICROSOFT FLIGHT SIMULATOR 2024

Microsoft Flight Simulator 2024 is looking to be one giant leap for the storied franchise. PC Gamer recently got to sit down with Jorge Neumann, head of Microsoft Flight Simulator, to show off a few show-stopping features that are generating excitement for the next game in the series.

Explore the World—On Foot

Among the other exciting new features is the option to leave the plane and explore the world on foot. Once landed, players can get out of the cockpit and walk wherever they want, whether it's hiking a scenic mountain trail, walking along a lakeside, or simply watching the sunset. This kind of freedom has never been seen before and adds a whole new dimension to the simulation.

And that's not all: Players will be able to make landings on ships-aircraft carriers, to be specific-and then stroll around as if they were playing a first-person shooter game. This element of the game brings the action out of the cockpit and delivers an interactive experience new to a flight simulator.

Unparalleled Realism in World Design

Asobo Studio is pushing the boundaries of realism with Bing Maps' topographic data. The team has taken that data and enhanced it even further with even greater attention to detail, with landscapes, flora, and fauna more realistic than ever before. Machine learning brings authenticity to the world, although it does require the occasional manual tweak-such as the removal of imaginary forests-to make the simulation flawless.

There were considerable revisions to environmental and weather conditions as well. The title uses real-time meteorological information-wind patterns, cloud cover, precipitation-to make every flight as dynamic and unpredictable as it is to fly in the real world.

Authentic Aircraft and Immersive Gameplay

Attention to realism extends to aircraft interiors as well: all cockpits and instrument panels have been carefully re-modeled in cooperation with the actual aircraft manufacturers to create an experience that's almost indistinguishable from flying a real aircraft.

Flight mechanics have also been fine-tuned to deliver intuitive and responsive controls, whether you're piloting a small propeller plane or a massive airliner. Every detail has been crafted to give players the most immersive and authentic flying experience possible.

A Story-Driven Flight Experience

Microsoft Flight Simulator 2024 will feature, for the first time in the series, a proper campaign mode. Unlike previous games that have no genuine narrative emphasis, the new mode will guide players on a journey across the world, providing a good sense of direction beyond simply flying from airport to airport.

With its combination of aerial and on-foot action, state-of-the-art realism, and compelling narrative, Microsoft Flight Simulator 2024 is bound to redefine the genre. Whether a veteran fan of flight or a newcomer, the possibilities for exploration and adventure are limitless. Strap yourself in as it hits the shelves on November 19th!

OPTIMIZE YOUR CONTROL SETTINGS

Before jumping headlong into Microsoft Flight Simulator 2024, take a moment to tweak your control settings for the optimal experience. It may take some trial and error to get the proper setup, but it will make a huge difference in how the game plays. Here's how to begin:

First, understand your controller type. Be it using a keyboard and mouse, an Xbox controller, a flight stick, or a complete flight setup, the methodology is vastly different.

Go to Options >> Control Options and select the default. Begin tweaking them to your personal taste from here.

Sensitivity settings are important. Try these starting sensitivity values:

- Pitch/Roll: -50% sensitivity
- Throttle: 0% sensitivity
- Rudder/Rotation: -20% sensitivity

You'll likely also want to reassign all of the key bindings to whatever you're most used to using in the. Control Options. Make small tweaks as you get more comfortable.

Engage it in Free Flight Mode. Finish any modification you want to do here.

Step Into Career Mode

The biggest addition to Microsoft Flight Simulator 2024 on Game Pass is the Career Mode. The other versions had been focused primarily on free flying, but this version has a more structured format in the form of career options. Players get the chance to enjoy various careers in aviation, such as:

- **Commercial Pilot** – Responsible for managing passenger flights and their schedules.
- **Bush Pilot** – Responsible for flying over difficult terrain and unexplored regions.
- **Air Ambulance/Rescue Pilot** – Respond to medical emergencies and evacuations.
- **Agricultural Pilot** – Perform crop-dusting and agricultural services.
- **Cargo Pilot** – Transport goods worldwide.
- **Charter/Private Pilot** – Fly exclusive clients to their destinations.
- **Helicopter Operations –** Take on specialized rotorcraft missions.

Each line of business has unique challenges, from making passengers smile to precision landings. If you don't want to commit a whole career, Aerial Work Missions are also on offer, where you can try out single career-based missions without a lifetime commitment.

Adjust Your Graphics Settings

Microsoft Flight Simulator 2024 is just as beautiful, yet system-intensive, as its counterpart. To refine the rough edges in this title, it takes tweaking those graphics settings.

- With a pretty current system, begin at medium and go higher gradually to high or ultra-based on what your hardware can sustain.
- More advanced levels of settings are remarkably detailed, but ultra will be taxing for anything short of the most extreme systems.
- Highlight adjusting your frame rate (FPS) for the best performance vs. visual quality.

Jump Into Multiplayer

Perhaps the most exciting aspect of Microsoft Flight Simulator 2024 is its multiplayer environment. If you want to share the skies with friends or take part in international events, there are plenty of options available.

Shared Skies Mode enables you to see real-time air traffic and interact with other players.

- Live Events (under the Event tab on the main menu) offer:
- Special Events: Air races, challenges, and milestone competitions.
- Community Events: Missions and activities designed by players.
- Seasonal Events: Themed activities associated with holidays or real-life aviation events.
- Receive news on upcoming events via the In-Game News Feed and Event Calendar (Activities in main menu).

On Foot Exploration

Most significantly new in Microsoft Flight Simulator 2024 is the feature to leave your aircraft and do some flying on foot. Whether strolling through an airport, hiking a mountain trail, or walking around a lakeside, this feature adds a whole new dimension to the game.

To the newbies, it's a whole different way of experiencing the game's, really, wonderful outdoors up close and personal-a feat no other flight simulator has achieved.

With all these enhancements, Microsoft Flight Simulator 2024 will be the most realistic one yet. Fine-tune your controls, reboot your career, and gaze out beyond the cockpit-there's a lot to take in.

REAL-WORLD TERRAIN AND LIVE WEATHER

MSFS 2024 will bring along some really sweet updates to its weather system-making the skies even more realistic and dynamic than before. Enhanced visuals, new weather phenomena, and more detailed gameplay mechanics are set to be a game-changer in flight simulation.

Breathtaking Cloud and Atmospheric Enhancements

The first thing you will notice in MSFS 2024 is the new presentation of clouds. With far more realistic, volumetric clouds, from wispy cirrus to towering thunderheads, it will now feel and look so much more realistic. If you fly with live weather turned on, that realism is another notch higher as clouds shift in density and shape naturally.

Of course, but another huge update has been done on the lighting engine. With the help of advanced ray tracing, MSFS 2024 now perfectly replicates how the sun behaves in the atmosphere-more smooth color changes during the day and more realistic changes in lighting at different altitudes, e.g., high-altitude clouds remaining lit up while those near the earth get darker during sunset. Lighting in MSFS 2024 is significantly more realistic with the addition of a new photometric lighting system that results in everything from brutal noon sun to the faint glimmer of city lights way in the distance being represented in accurate intensity and temperature.

New Weather Phenomena: Tornadoes, Northern Lights & More

Aurora Borealis – The stunning Northern Lights finally make their appearance in the game on certain dates. Players can change the in-game date to enjoy this beautiful work of nature.

Tornadoes – Presently available in certain limited missions only, they intend to incorporate them into live weather in the near future. Live data is being collected by the developers so as to provide storm chasing a very dynamic experience.

Wildfires: More authentic through the deployment of an updated cloud system, MSFS 2024 visualizes fire smoke and fog to put an end to the heartbreaking firefighting mission. The inclement weather decreases visibility, enhancing the emergency response mission further.

Seasons & Biomes: Seasonal dynamic with seasons using 23 diverse biomes. Leaves turning colors in the autumn, snowflakes falling on runways, and searing heat waves during summer aren't only pleasant visuals. Snow and ice impair takeoff performance, and hot air from summers creates massive thermals to challenge glider pilots.

Improved Fog & Visibility Simulation - Fog on the ground, pollution layers, and temperature inversions now act a great deal more realistic. Low-vis conditions have never been more realistic.

HOW WEATHER IMPACTS FLIGHT DYNAMICS

MSFS 2024 is not just about prettier weather; it actually governs how planes should behave. The new Computational Fluid Dynamics (CFD) system in the simulator improves simulating wind and turbulence. Wake turbulence from other planes can be up to six minutes, and mountain updrafts and ridge lift are much more realistic to fly in gliders and light aircraft.

Other significant improvements are:

- Enhanced turbulence effects, weather dependent.
- Takeoff and landing wind effects have been optimized for realism.
- Precipitation physics influence aircraft performance, from ice runways to compromised efficiency of engines in moist air.
- New rotor wash particle effects enhance the capabilities of helicopters to churn up dust and grass.

Functional windshield wipers: Wet-weather flying just became a whole lot more realistic, since functional wipers enable pilots to be able to see through rain.

Give your flying an extra level of realism with the 24-hour historical weather option, which enables you to backdate to the weather of twelve months prior, as part of enhanced multi-leg flights and flight planning.

Performance & Technical Improvements

But even with this added realism, MSFS 2024 has been tuned for butter-smooth performance. Detailed weather effects, such as wake turbulence, now make use of multi-threaded processing to alleviate the strain on your system somewhat. Effects that scale mean that lower-end systems can still enjoy playing the game, but top-of-the-range systems can immerse themselves in fully ultra-realistic conditions.

In-flight planner sees an update that will enable pilots to see forecasted weather along flight paths. As it stands, due to MSFS 2024 moving to a cloud-based weather system, this will be updated and refined more often than previously to keep the simulation current and new.

A Living, Breathing Atmosphere

More of it means that with all this creation, MSFS 2024 does not necessarily model flight as much as it is a real-time, live world responding to the world outside in real time. From stormy turbulence from thunderstorms to chasing tornadoes or simply relaxing at sunset altitude 30,000 feet high, the sky has never lived so much.

Having spent the time, I have with it since the Global Preview Event, it is clear how Microsoft and Asobo responded to the cries of the community and have delivered on a revolutionary weather system. This is not an update; this is flying differently.

This one keeps the important information, though in a friendlier tone, and puts the text more beautifully and in an easier format. If you desire any additional adjustments, please let me know!

CITIES AIRPORTS AND LANDSCAPES

How do you take a great flight simulator and make it a great flight simulation game?

That's the question at the heart of Microsoft Flight Simulator 2024, the latest iteration of the classic series-one that now tries to please both hard-core flying enthusiasts and more casual gamers alike, including those who discover it through Xbox Game Pass. It's almost like Asobo Studio is trying to find a middle ground between these two poles of experience: an über-realistic flight simulator where an experienced pilot can flip every toggle switch on an Airbus A310 and a friendly, controller-oriented experience with generous assists to educate new players on takeoff, cruise, and landing. But lost in these ambitions, I'm back to the same question: Why am I flying? There's no sense of motion to speak of, no blindingly beautiful visual display, and an annoying fear that at some point some fly-by-night bug will send my experience careening into some sort of inadvertent nose-dive. At best, MSFS 2024 is a fantastic, 8.5-out-of-10 flight simulation.

Without even grasping a gamepad, in-game aids allow takeoff, flight, and landing a light aircraft with the real feel.

You can fly pretty much anywhere in the world-even through prohibited areas like North Korea's. The game runs fairly well on Xbox Series X and even better on high-performance gaming computers, rendering high-definition clouds, lush landscapes, and familiar cities. If you feel up to taking immersion to new heights, you can attach a full HOTAS setup, eye-tracking gear, or even a VR headset. This iteration enhances the foundation Microsoft Flight Simulator (2020) set, in which Asobo and Microsoft touted a fully explorable world with cutting-edge visuals and Bing mapping data. In its initial launch, that iteration delivered realistic scenes from high heights but didn't cut it close up—Blurry cities, lifeless landscape, and oceans that weren't always realistic. In MSFS 2024, it is much better. At around 10,000 feet, the world looks a whole lot more realistic because of improved foliage rendering and generally more realistic-looking forests. The procedural generation of terrain remains, though, a bit off. Vast areas of the world-a strip of land in Mexico-are weird, blotchy textures that are more suitable to an early 2000s Ace Combat game than to a new flight sim.

Asobo Studio/Xbox Game Studios

As in MSFS 2020, large cities and airports in MSFS 2024 still utilize handcrafted models for famous landmarks. Think of famous landmarks like the Eiffel Tower, the New York City skyline, and Christ the Redeemer in Brazil-these all look essentially the same as their previous incarnations. Unfortunately, the same can be said of the majority of the many lower-priority buildings as well, making a lot of cities look generic and visual messes.

Take Dallas, for example—my hometown and an important international city. The only landmark they've gotten correct is the basketball and hockey arena, and it's not even near the downtown skyline. Meanwhile, the two prominent Calatrava bridges in the city are still represented as generic roads crossing a river, with only white concrete where their iconic arches should be. If you were flying by visual flight rules (VFR), you would far rather see accurately scaled bridges than a highly detailed stadium.

Asobo Studio/Xbox Game Studios

The real issue with MSFS 2024 is how often it teeters between breathtaking realism and distracting imperfections. One moment, you're soaring through a stunning sunset, with the sky painted in rich oranges and purples, and clouds so lifelike they could belong on a postcard. But then, a little further down, the forms of an island resemble chunky Duplo blocks, its shoreline sports some awkward wave effects, and a garish seam between land and sea cries out loudly. Zoom out further, and in an instant your plane dazzles with texture issues-distracting from tree-lined mountain majesty that should take pride of place in the distance.

At altitude or from the take-off of one of the well-designed airports of the game, MSFS 2024 evades most of its visual problems. For others who just wish to fly within the sim, their HOTAS attached and prepared, it is an acceptable experience, whether this flight is a 20-minute or an 80-minute trip. For the fun gamer, though, one perhaps much happy to simply enjoy the view, that is more difficult to accomplish with looks this inconsistent.

MSFS 2024 tries to stage scenes for gamers in a more impressive manner and gives them a sense of fulfillment with a set of new activities. That sounds great on paper, but isn't quite so in reality.

Video games struggle to represent a whole planet. No Man's Sky had infinite procedural worlds, but its formal gameplay elements—like missions and base-building—overpowered its vast, empty landscapes. Spore promised galactic exploration but had players working with dead planets that were repetitive in an instant.

One game that did it right? Where in the World Is Carmen Sandiego? It utilized real-world locations and brought them to life with puzzles, history, and narrative. MSFS 2024 is the opposite of Carmen Sandiego.

Its "activities" are hidden in a main menu and frequently require finesse and precision to execute. Some of them reward you for flying as low as you can without crashing, and others require you to land in terrible weather on tiny runways. But the game does not encourage players to use the extensive flight-training exercises it offers them prior to attempting such activities—including exercises that actually constitute mandatory training.

The most obvious activity is a series of photography challenges, where you soar towards famous landmarks, half-fly there, and snap a certain type of shot. The first challenge? Photographing the pyramids. Sounds like a cool, only-in-video-games experience—until you zoom in and notice the poorly rendered structures and blotchy textures. And then you can't help but wonder: Did anyone actually playtest this feature? Of all the locations to start, was this really what the developers wanted the players to be introduced with first?

Asobo Studio/Xbox Game Studios

At altitude or departing the game's exquisitely modeled airports, MSFS 2024 avoids most of its graphical problems. For pilots who just like to fly in the sim, HOTAS mounted and ready to go, it's a positive experience, whether that's an 80-minute flight or a 20-minute one. For the casual player, though, one who might be more likely to simply take in the views, that's more difficult when the graphics are this inconsistent

MSFS 2024 tries to frame scenes more for players and gives them a sense of achievement with a whole bunch of new activities. That sounds good on paper, but plays out less so in execution.

Video games struggle to represent an entire planet. No Man's Sky had limitless procedural worlds, but its more structured gameplay elements—like missions and base-building—dwarfed its endless, empty landscapes. Spore promised galactic travel but had players managing dead planets that quickly became repetitive.

One game that did get it right? Where in the World Is Carmen Sandiego? It took real-world locations and brought them to life with puzzles, history, and storytelling. MSFS 2024, by contrast, is the anti-Carmen Sandiego.

Its "activities" are buried in a primary menu and typically demand precision and finesse to complete. Some missions reward you for flying as low as possible without crashing, but others challenge you to land in atrocious weather on minuscule runways. But the game does not push players toward the comprehensive flight-training exercises it has available before trying such activities—exercises that amount to mandatory training, effectively.

Most gimmicky is a series of photography challenges, wherein players fly towards famous landmarks, freeze in mid-air, and snap a specific type of photograph. The first challenge? Getting a shot of the pyramids. It's got all the ingredients of an thrilling, video-games-only moment—until you zoom in and notice the poorly rendered buildings and muddled textures. At which point, you can't help but wonder: Did anybody even test this feature? Of all the places to start, was this really what the developers wanted the players to see first?

On first blush, MSFS24's new "career" mode is a promising feature, where gamers can evolve from greenhorn pilot to aviation tycoon. The intent is to start with initial flight training, get certified, take on more and more challenging missions, and eventually buy aircraft and run a company. There is lots of activity on offer-rescue operations, air firefighting, and skydiving operations-but in practice, the experience is fragmented or agonizingly flat.

The issue is, it relies so heavily on AI-generated content, essentially stripping the game of any attempt at real storytelling. Instead of beautifully crafted scenarios, missions will certainly sound more like meaningless and uncaring tasks. Passengers are automated; speaking in stiff, mechanical voices as vacantly staring from their seats. The dialog can be so wooden at times you find yourself wishing you wreck the plane just to get out of having to hear it.

And even not factoring in the weirdness of AI, the infrastructure beneath is one maddening design decision after another: since the missions are designed to happen all over the globe at random, sometimes these takeoff and landing points end up being absurd locations that actually have trees and buildings right in front of you. As heartless as career mode's economy, in which it takes bites out of your hard-earned cash for even minor mistakes, halting any forward momentum you gained significantly. Since you have to pay to earn new certifications, a single hard landing will leave you far behind. Worse yet are the mission objectives that are unclear or buggy. Sometimes taking shortcuts gets you paid in full as well, but jumping ahead on a mission will cause critical flight systems to malfunction, so it is not feasible to be able to do things like talk to air traffic control. The game has you buy your own plane as you proceed.

But if a glitch in the runway sends your plane careening out of control, you're off for expensive repairs or full replacement value. Same with AI pilots you hire: send them on missions and you'll be facing surprise bills with no real rhyme or reason why. Even if these are addressed in future patches, it's surprising the game does not have a simple feature to loosen up career mode's economy. All of this, of course, does not touch on the underlying flight simulation dynamics that hardcore aficionado might discuss. Over more than 30 hours of play, I endured constant bugs, career progression bottlenecks, and even a strange glitch where hot air balloons released heat in reverse - a patch that would've incinerated passengers in the real world. Discovering MSFS24 making deicing procedures much too complex in the real world came from watching a real pilot play on Twitch. Instead of a smooth, rewarding flight simulation ride, MSFS24 is full of random-shot tutorials, lumbering career arcs, and disillusionment on the eye. Deliberately assembled AI-generated content has given rise to plainer created landmarks and bridges. Even setting up the flight stick is a chore-the game offers no instructions to it, making me take an entire page of manual down to figure out controls. My emails to Microsoft's PR division for help? Crickets.

The issues are guaranteed to be solved if Asobo continues at the same rate as the MSFS20 update cycle.

But based on the history of Microsoft-just consider how Halo Infinite petered out in no time-I wouldn't trust them with everything.

However, you can go ahead with MSFS24 if all you want is "more of the good stuff from MSFS20". But the fundamental design issues of the game cannot be addressed with bandaids, and too many players already acted as beta testers for a title that costs full price. If you're not already deeply invested in flight sims, MSFS24 isn't worth the money.

CUSTOMIZING YOUR FLIGHT EXPERIENCE

Much-awaited Microsoft Flight Simulator 2024 by Asobo Studio, published by Xbox Game Studios, arrives on November 19, 2024. This release sets new standards for flight simulation using the latest technology, stunning realism, and deep immersion.

Whether you're a fan of flight sims or just have a passing interest in flying, this is one game to which you owe some attention.

What's New in Microsoft Flight Simulator 2024?

A True Pilot's Career

MSFS 2024 introduces the career mode. From a novice pilot, you can thus ascend the ranks to become an experienced aviator. Fly medevac missions, cargo transport, or combat wildfires from the air-the challenge never stops.

Next-Level Realism

The new physics engine of the game includes more than 10,000 rigid-body surfaces and soft-body physics, making every flight highly realistic.

Exciting Challenges

Test your abilities with rally races, precision landings, low-level obstacle courses, and even historic air races like the Red Bull and Reno Air Races.

World Photographer Mode

Capture breathtaking scenery, iconic landmarks, and hidden gems with special photo challenges designed specifically for aviation photographers.

Real-Time Weather & Seasons

Experience the variability of actual snow, actual tornadoes, actual aurora, and more in dynamic seasons that do affect your flight.

Enormous Aircraft Fleet

MSFS 2024 offers an immense fleet of richly detailed planes, from legacy aircraft to the latest jets, including the De Havilland Canada CL-415 aerial firefighter.

Multiplayer & VR Compatibility

Soar with friends or put on your headset and go virtual for a flying experience unlike any other.

EDITIONS & AIRCRAFT AVAILABILITY

✈ Standard Edition – 70 Aircraft, 150 Airports

✈ Deluxe Edition – 80 Aircraft, 155 Airports

✈ Premium Deluxe Edition – 95 Aircraft, 160 Airports

✈ Aviator Edition – 125 Aircraft, 160 Airports

Take to the skies in the version that best fits your flying ambitions!

System Requirements

Below are the system requirements for running MSFS 2024 smoothly:

☑ CPU: AMD Ryzen 5 2600X / Intel Core i7-6800K or better

☑ RAM: 16GB

☑ Graphics: AMD Radeon RX 5700 / NVIDIA GeForce GTX 970 or better

☑ VRAM: 4GB

☑ Storage: 50GB

☑ Internet: 10 Mbps connection

☑ OS: Windows 10 (latest update)

Tips for New Pilots

Master flight controls, takeoffs, and landings. Smooth: Avoid making jerky motion to maintain control. Customize Your Controls: Tailor controls, view, and sensitivity to your play style. Choose the Appropriate Plane: Acquire an airplane that is suited to your playing style: whether it is a passenger airliner, freight aircraft, or fighter plane.

Learn One Plane On A Time: Don't overdo it, just learn one plane initially.

Begin with Short Flights: Raise your confidence level before attempting long flights.

Turn on Unlimited Fuel: This removes any stress of fuel depletion when you are learning.

Utilize the Toolbar: Familiarize yourself with all the in-game tools that will make flying a breeze.

Microsoft Flight Simulator 2024 will be the most realistic flight simulator, combining realism, career play, and breathtaking scenery in a completely unbelievable way. Regardless of what your flying passion is, casual or in hardcore aviation devotion-there is something for you.

So, buckle up because this is about to get real on a whole new scale! 🛩️

CHAPTER 4

MASTERING AIRCRAFT CONTROLS

Your first few flights in Microsoft Flight Simulator 2024 can be daunting, as there's a long list of keyboard controls that you'll need to commit to memory. Even experienced sim pilots will find themselves searching for the right key-some of these controls differ from MSFS 2020.

If you're struggling to keep track of all the commands, don't worry! Two great resources on Flightsim.to can help simplify things and make flying much smoother.

Your Go-To Keyboard Guide

One of the most useful tools is "Default MSFS 2024 All Keyboard Commands." This guide provides a complete breakdown of every shortcut in the game, neatly organized into categories like:

🛩 **Camera Controls**: Toggle your view with ease.

Navigation & Flight Management: On track with ease.

⚙️ **Engine & System Controls**: Manage power, fuel, and avionics with ease.

Having this guide next to you will have you spending less time trying to find that one key and more time taking in the flight.

I am simply having trouble coming up with a point of reference in the form of MSFS 2024's three categories of peripheral configurations:

Someone detail them all in good stead. How might one easiest go about making control profiles for even classes of airplanes-and even planes per se? It all is beginning to sound hinky, so just about any practical advice would surely be much appreciated.

MSFS 2024 Keyboard Commands

CAMERA		
Toggle Auto Exposure	2	SHIFT + F4
Toggle Auto Focus	1	F4
Exposure Decrease	G	SHIFT + F2
Exposure Increase	T	SHIFT + F3
Focus Decrease	F	SHIFT + F6
Focus Increase	R	SHIFT + F7
Take Picture	SPACE	
Zoom Out	SHIFT + U	-
Zoom In	SHIFT + O	+
Pan Left	J	LEFT
Pan Right	L	RIGHT
Pitch Down	K	DOWN
Pitch Up	I	UP
Roll Left	U	
Roll Right	O	
Reset Horizon	SHIFT + SPACE	
Photo Mode Toggle	SHIFT + V	
Move Backward	S	
Move Down	Q	
Move Forward	W	
Move Left	A	
Move Right	D	
Move Up	E	

LIGHTS		
Toggle Lights	;	
Toggle Flashlight	ALT + F	

POWER MANAGEMENT		
Condition Lever Cut Off	CTRL + H	F9
Decrease Condition Lever	H	F10
Condition Lever High Idle	CTRL + Y	F12
Increase Condition Lever	Y	F11
Decrease Mixture	H	F10
Increase Mixture	Y	F11
Set Mixture Lean	CTRL + H	F9
Set Mixture Rich	CTRL + Y	F12
Decrease Propeller Pitch	G	F6
Propeller Pitch HI	CTRL + G	F5
Increase Propeller Pitch	T	F7
Propeller Pitch LO	CTRL + T	F8
Throttle Next Detent	CTRL + R	F4
Throttle Previous Detent	CTRL + F	F1
Decrease Throttle	F	F2
Increase Throttle	R	F3

FLIGHT CONTROL SURFACES		
Aileron Trim Left	J	CTRL + NUM 4
Aileron Trim Right	L	CTRL + NUM 6
Elevator Trim Down (Nose Down)	I	NUM 7
Elevator Trim Up (Nose Up)	K	NUM 1
Rudder Trim Left	U	CTRL + NUM 0
Rudder Trim Right	O	CTRL + NUM DEL
Decrease Flaps	V	
Extend Flaps	CTRL + B	
Increase Flaps	B	
Retract Flaps	CTRL + V	
Toggle Arm Spoilers	CTRL + \	
Increment Spoilers	N	
Decrement Spoilers	M	
Retract Spoilers	CTRL + N	
Extend Spoilers	CTRL + M	
Aileron Left (Roll Left)	A	NUM 4
Aileron Right (Roll Right)	D	NUM 6
Center Aileron Rudder	NUM 5	
Elevator Down (Pitch Down)	W	NUM 8
Elevator Up (Pitch Up)	S	NUM 2
Center Rudder	CTRL + Q	
Rudder Left (Yaw Left)	Q	NUM 0
Rudder Right (Yaw Right)	E	NUM DEL
Toggle Water Rudder	CTRL + /	

INSTRUMENTS AND SYSTEM		
Toggle Master Battery and Alternator	CTRL + Z	
Toggle Anti Ice	'	
Set Magnetos	CTRL + C	
Toggle AutoRudder	CTRL + P	
Toggle Avionics Master	CTRL + X	
Select Airspeed Bug	CTRL + 3	
Select Altitude Bug	CTRL + 4	
Select Heading Bug	CTRL + 5	
Select VSI Bug	CTRL + 6	
Toggle Tail Hook Handle	CTRL + /	

BRAKES		
Toggle Parking Brakes	CTRL + SPACE	
Brakes	SPACE	
Left Brake	NUM /	
Right Brake	NUM *	

AUTOPILOT		
Autopilot Airspeed Hold		CTRL + F1
Toggle Autopilot Altitude Hold		CTRL + F2
Decrease Autopilot Reference Altitude		CTRL + PAGE DOWN
Increase Autopilot Reference Altitude		CTRL + PAGE UP
Toggle Autopilot Approach Hold		CTRL + F3
Toggle Autopilot Attitude Hold		CTRL + F4
Toggle Autopilot Flight Level Change		CTRL + F9
Toggle Autopilot Heading Hold		CTRL + F5
Toggle Autopilot Localizer Hold		CTRL + F10
Toggle Autopilot Mach Hold		CTRL + F11
Toggle Autopilot Master		CTRL + 1
Toggle Disengage Autopilot		CTRL + 2
Autopilot N1 Hold		CTRL + F6
Decrease Autopilot N1 Reference		CTRL + END
Increase Autopilot N1 Reference		CTRL + HOME
Set Autopilot N1 Reference		CTRL + 8
Autopilot NAV1 Hold		CTRL + F7
Decrease Autopilot Reference Airspeed		CTRL + DEL
Increase Autopilot Reference Airspeed		CTRL + INSERT
Toggle Autopilot VS Hold		CTRL + F8
Decrease Autopilot Reference VS		CTRL + END
Increase Autopilot Reference VS		CTRL + HOME
Toggle Autopilot Wing Leveler		CTRL + F12
Arm Auto Throttle		CTRL + [
Autothrottle Disconnect		CTRL + '
Auto Throttle to GA		CTRL +]
Toggle G Limiter		Z

PLAYER CHARACTER		
Take Control of Character	SHIFT + C	
Interact	E	NUM 9
Look Down	K	DOWN
Look Left	J	LEFT
Camera Reset	SHIFT + SPACE	
Look Right	L	RIGHT
Look Up	I	UP
Toggle Crouch	C	NUM 1
Move Backward	S	NUM 2
Move Forward	W	NUM 8
Strafe Left	A	NUM 4
Strafe Right	D	NUM 6
Toggle Run	SPACE	NUM 3

LANDING GEAR		
Toggle Landing Gear	/	

Easy access to keyboard commands

No more groping in the dark for the correct key! It doesn't even matter whether you're using a dark or light theme; this is a keyboard shortcut guide made easy for you to refer to. Print it out and keep it as a constant companion, and put it on a second monitor where you can easily glance at it at a glance! No more guessing complicated key combinations, just nicely formatted data right in front of your eyes!

◉ Get the entire guide here.

A Visual Shortcut Map for Quick Navigation

If you are a visual learner, the "Keyboard Layout with Default MSFS 2024 Commands" is another great option. This color-coded map graphs all the key shortcuts onto a typical QWERTY keyboard, allowing you to quickly locate:

- Throttle & Engine Controls
- Camera Adjustments
- Autopilot Functions

With distinct colors highlighting key features, you'll be able to spot commands at a glance—no more hunting for the right keys mid-flight!

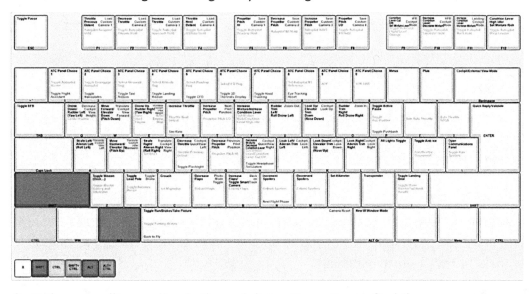

Don't sit there scrolling endlessly through lists attempting to find the command you require; glance across at the keyboard layout and there it is. What does the P key do? There on the chart is the answer: it activates Active Pause, and in combination with ALT it activates pushback.

Getting Started with Microsoft Flight Simulator 2024

With its complexity and depth, Microsoft Flight Simulator 2024 features an incredible range of features-but navigating them effectively is the trick. These keyboard guides will help you:

✓ Master controls more quickly

✓ Save time and frustration

✓ Concentrate on flying-not searching for keys

From the experienced pilot to the novice newcomer, these ready-reference tools will make flight easier, more fun, and immersive. 🛩

BASICS OF FLIGHT CONTROLS AND INSTRUMENTS

Adjusting to a new sim always takes time, and Microsoft Flight Simulator 2024 is no different. With the game having just been released last week, most simmers are diving into its new control layout—full of robust customization options but a few stumbling blocks to work through.

If you've wasted hours gazing at the settings menu, cursing under your breath that something just isn't quite right, don't worry - you're among friends. Hours have been wasted by many a player twiddling controls in a desperate bid to get everything remapped perfectly.

The bad news? Beneath the bewildering interface lies a more flexible and powerful system than ever. Once you've mastered it, setting up your controls can actually be gratifying—well, almost!

A Helpful Guide

To make it easy, Jonathan Beckett's new You Tube video walks you through the new system in a clear and handy way. If you're finding the revamped control settings in MSFS 2024 tricky, it's well worth watching.

What's New in MSFS 2024

As Jonathan depicts, the control system has been completely overhauled. Instead of a single profile per device as before, MSFS 2024 separates controls into three categories:

- **General Controls** – Manages simulator-wide operations like navigating menus and camera views.
- **Airplane Controls** – Manages critical flight controls like throttle, ailerons, and rudder.
- **Specific Controls** – Regulates specific aircraft operations, including helicopter winches or jet afterburners.

This setup provides for more comprehensive personalization, especially for special-handling airplanes. Although the new system can seem daunting at first, it starts to make sense after adjusting to it.

Using the Controls Menu

You can invoke the controls menu in several ways:

- From the Main Menu, go to Control Options.
- Press Esc in mid-flight and select Controls.
- Use the Controls pop-up window at the top of the toolbar while in flight.

Your aircraft is shown at the top, and attached devices are shown on the left upon entry. Click on a device, and its settings will become available where you can filter controls to display assigned functions only or see all available mappings.

A good starting point is to use the Assigned filter, which shows you only the controls that are already mapped to your device. This will give you an immediate overview of what's already working and what might need tweaking—without being overwhelmed by an ocean of unmapped options.

Setting Up and Managing Control Profiles

All of the aircraft within MSFS 2024 include a default profile, to which you are unable to change or rename it. Instead, whenever you do tweak settings, MSFS builds you a custom profile. It's here, where naming straightforwardly matters-using something like "Basic Throttle and Mixture" for a Cessna 172 or "Twin Engine Jet" for a more sophisticated setup truly simplifies changing profiles.

Additionally, Jonathan Beckett's video illustrates how you can duplicate, rename and then utilize profiles on various aircraft. This is a must-have for anyone who alternates between multiple different planes and needs a customized control scheme on each.

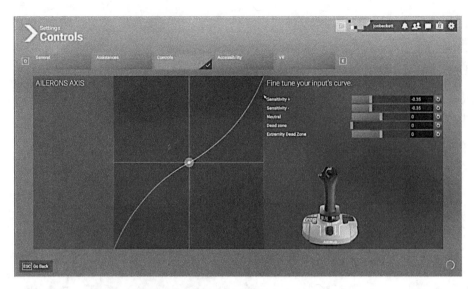

Fine-Tuning Sensitivity for Greater Control

One of the most helpful aspects of MSFS 2024 is the ability to modify sensitivity curves on a per-control basis.

To accomplish this:

1. Click on the Hardware Settings option, which is located underneath the controller image.

2. Adjust the way your inputs respond with the sliders or number values.

For example:

- Flattening the middle of the curve allows for smoother throttle inputs.
- A more sloping curve can bring precision to control surfaces like ailerons and rudders.
- Beckett shows how adjusting these can make all the difference in responsiveness, depending on the type of aircraft you are flying.

Automatic Profile Selection

One of the nice enhancements in MSFS 2024 is that this simulator now recalls your custom profiles. Suppose you've just created a custom control profile on a Cessna 172, the next time you'll be flying that plane, the sim will load that profile for you automatically, saving yourself the misery of having to switch profiles every single time.

Getting Familiar with New System

The Control Customization screen looks overwhelming at first, but once you've familiarized yourself with it, this control setup procedure is actually pretty straightforward. However, if you do have difficulty then Jonathan Beckett's walk-through video is an absolutely fantastic guide as far as familiarizing yourself with the new system.

Additional help can be found from MSFS' Support page where a more technical guide awaits.

By the time you've explored these tools, you'll have a solid grasp of how to fine-tune your controls—and might even appreciate just how much flexibility MSFS 2024 offers in personalizing your flight experience!

HOW TO TAKE OFF AND LAND SMOOTHLY

When it was released, Microsoft Flight Simulator 2024 had some pretty annoying server issues that frustrated players stuck loading screens. A couple patches on and the glitches disappear, stability kicks in, so players can now take to the skies and discover what this beautiful terrain has to offer.

But flying is only half the war-landing is where it gets tricky. Taking off is hardly a science, while landing a plane safely entails precision, patience, and some knowledge of aerodynamics. Courtesy of MSFS 2024's realistic simulator, a miscalculated landing can very quickly turn into disaster. In this tutorial, we will walk you through the three critical stages of landing: approach, slowing down, and braking, leading you to a smooth, safe landing at your destination airport.

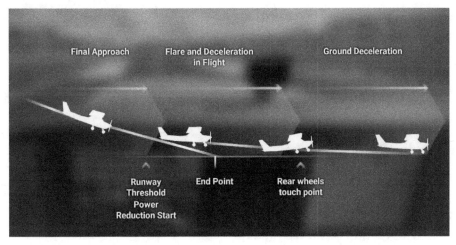

Step 1: The Approach

The approach phase is the manner in which you set yourself up for landing successfully. This is when you're still flying, coming onto the runway.

Most critical guidelines for a clean procedure:

☑ **Provide yourself with plenty of space** – Begin by slowly losing altitude with the runway in view.

☑ **Line up on the runway** – Use the rudder to center yourself (Q/E on PC, LT/RT on Xbox).

☑ **Manage your speed** – Slowly cut back your throttle to bring your speed to 100 KTAS or lower (F on PC, B on Xbox).

☑ **Keep your descent steady** – Adjust your angle smoothly to avoid an abrupt drop.

☑ **Lower your landing gear** – Press Forward Slash (/) on PC, Right D-Pad on Xbox to deploy your gear before touchdown.

Step 2: Deceleration & Flare

Once you're just above the runway, it's time to slow down further and prepare for touchdown.

How to decelerate effectively:

☑ Let go of your throttle completely (F on PC, B on Xbox).

☑ **Use detents if needed** – Depending on aircraft type, it may need to set it to idle power using CTRL + F (PC) or RB + B (Xbox).

☑ **Drop flaps to slow down** – Press B (PC) or Down on the D-Pad (Xbox) to bring them halfway down.

Flare: Final Adjustment Prior to Touchdown

Flare is the final adjustment prior to touchdown. Moments before your wheels kiss the ground:

☑ **Gradually ease the nose upward** - Keep it slightly above the horizon to act as a shock absorber.

☑ **Don't yank too hard** - Hard pull-up will stall the aircraft.

☑ **Land smoothly -** Rear wheels first, then the nose gear.

Step 3: Braking and Taxiing

Landing finally ends by bringing the plane to a stop.

☑ **Touch down smoothly** - Let the nose landing gear softly touch down on the runway.

☑ **Apply brakes gradually -** Press Space Bar (PC) or X (Xbox) to slow down, but do not slam the brakes hard to avoid nosing forward of the plane.

✔ **Controlled braking.**

Gradual braking: Brake periodically by pressing-relax, reapplying and accelerating to descend in an orderly manner to last speed.

taxi to park: From stop condition-follow ATC instructions taxi to your assigned parking spot or finish your flight operation.

A smooth landing isn't just about touching down—it's about coming to a controlled stop and handling your aircraft properly on the ground. With practice, you'll perfect the art of landing in MSFS 2024!

UNDERSTANDING AUTOPILOT AND NAVIGATION SYSTEMS

With Microsoft Flight Simulator 2024 mirroring real-world flight durations, long-haul trips can take hours. That's where autopilot comes in handy. However, unlike a simple "auto-fly" button, MSFS 2024 requires manual setup—just like a real aircraft. If you're unsure how to activate and manage autopilot, this guide will break it down step by step.

Activating Autopilot (AP)

1. Lift off and level your airspeed and attitude.
2. Click the AP button, usually beside the Primary Flight Display.

3. Select your target altitude with the ALT wheel.
4. Choose what kind of climb you want to do:
   - VS Mode (Vertical Speed) – Changes attitude by pitching the nose up or down.
   - FLC Mode (Flight Level Change) – Altitude correction with airspeed.

5. **Choose a navigation mode:**
   - NAV Mode – The GPS flight plan will be followed.
   - HDG Mode – You manually set and change the heading.

Autopilot Essentials

Controls are essentially the same with minor differences on various aircraft; the core autopilot functions remain constant. The three important ones include:

Heading, HDG Mode Keeps the plane flying in one direction. Make an adjustment with the HDG wheel. Convenient if you're not pre-loading a flight plan into.

Navigation (NAV Mode): Automatically follows your GPS path of flight. Without a flight plan, touch the "Nearest" button and look up an airport in the area and select it.

Altitude Management (ALT Mode): Controls your level of altitude.

Vertical Speed (VS): Changes altitude by adjusting the pitch of the nose. Use the Nose Up/Nose Down keys to control climb or descent.

Flight Level Change (FLC): Altitude adjustment according to flight speed. Input a target speed in knots, and it will control the climb or descent for you.

These are the autopilot changes that you will have to make flying more efficient, decrease work during long-haul flights, and make smoother rides in Microsoft Flight Simulator 2024! ✈️

Possible Fixes for Autopilot Not Working

If autopilot isn't engaging, it's likely due to one of the following problems:

CDI Not Set to GPS – If your aircraft is not on the flight plan, check the Course Deviation Indicator (CDI). Press the CDI button on the Primary Flight Display until it changes to GPS mode—you will see magenta bars rather than green.

✦ OBS Mode is On - Autopilot will not function when OBS, or Omni Bearing Selector, is active. Don't forget to switch it off prior to activating autopilot.

✦ Throttle Set Incorrectly - Some aircraft, such as the majority of the Airbus series, like the throttle to be in CL or Climb position. Otherwise, the autopilot will not respond.

By checking these settings, you'll be able to activate autopilot and enjoy a smoother flight in Microsoft Flight Simulator 2024! ✈️

CHAPTER 5

ADVANCED FLIGHT TECHNIQUES

What a time to be an enthusiast of flight sims! Ever since its release all the way back in 2020, Microsoft Flight Simulator has been upping the realism ante, and MSFS 2024 carries on in even greater fashion.

Navigraph's powerful set of tools is going to enrich your flights even further, with more depth in planning and navigation, and thus more realism. Recreational flyer or extreme virtual pilot, be what you are, a subscription with Navigraph equates to real-world flight charts, newer airways, and detailed navigation information directly into MSFS 2024.

Charts for Every Pilot

Regardless of how experienced you are, Navigraph gives you real-world, ready-to-use aeronautical charts that make you feel professional pilot-like. Whatever it is a complex IFR route you are flying or simply desire enhanced situational awareness; these charts really add a touch of realism to your flights.

Even more exciting ways Navigraph is improving the AI of MSFS 2024 will be announced in due course.

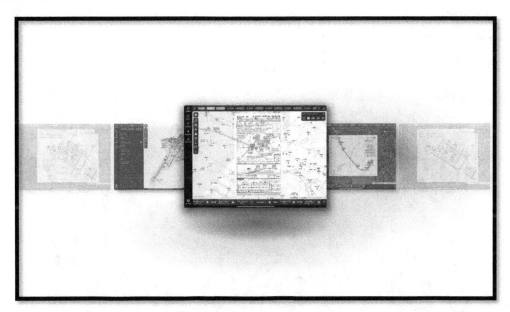

Navigraph has been the industry leader in providing aeronautical charts to flight sim enthusiasts for more than twenty years. We joined forces with Jeppesen, the leading provider of real-world aviation charts globally, in 2016 to offer the flight simulation world the best quality navigation data. Whether you're flying a Cessna 172 or an Airbus A380, our charts support all classes of aircraft types so that each virtual pilot has a comfortable journey.

Unparalleled Worldwide Coverage

Jeppesen's deep real-world network indicates that if an airport has been published instrument procedures, it's most likely to be found in Navigraph Charts. No provider can possibly cover all airports, but Jeppesen is the industry standard for full world coverage. Don't take our word on it—compare for yourself on our Airport Listing page.

Live Air Traffic & Real-Time Flight Data

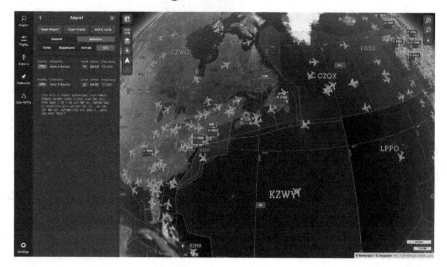

VATSIM and IVAO users can look forward to the ultimate realism boost with Navigraph, offering real-time air traffic data integrated into the app to track other aircraft, coordinate with approaches, and find your way more effectively through busy airspace. Plus, if flying into one of the over 1,000 supported AMDB airports, you'll have detailed all arrival, departure, and even gate availability information.

Always Up-To-Date Navigation Information

Experienced flight simmers appreciate the importance of up-to-date navigation data. Navigraph offers comprehensive SID/STAR procedures, airways, en-route waypoints, and transition points, just like in professional aviation. And the best part is, we update this data monthly in parallel with the official AIRAC cycle, so your flight plans are always accurate and realistic. We are proud of our reliability—Navigraph has never failed to update its navigation data over 20 years!

Intelligent Tools for Better Flight Planning

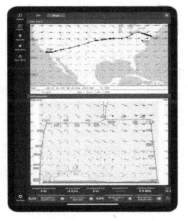

Navigraph is not just charts. Our features continue to grow and encompass:

✔ Enhanced weather layers showing real-time atmospheric conditions

✔ VFR charts with highly detailed graphics for ultra-precise navigation

✔ Tight integration with SimBrief for ultra-realistic flight planning

✔ Native iOS and Android apps so you can monitor flights on the move

At Navigraph, we're not only developers but also flight simmers ourselves. We listen to your feedback, and most of our in-app features were requested by our community at some point or another. We're honored to create the best experience we can for virtual pilots around the globe.

EMERGENCY PROCEDURES AND TROUBLESHOOTING

We're developing Microsoft Flight Simulator 2024, and we understand that most of our users are migrating from MSFS 2020. We've been successful in converting a lot of marketplace content but discovered that some third-party add-ons are troublesome— troubles that range from crashing on load into the game overall.

To avoid huge-scale problems, we've temporarily disabled all non-aircraft content from MSFS 2020 within MSFS 2024. We are rolling out a fix and as part of an upcoming patch, due to go live during the week of December 9th, we'll be including player options to manually enable/disable content. We'll also include a safe boot mode to help recover from third-party add-on crashes.

Xbox Series X|S: Current Issues & Fixes

Game Crash or Freeze when Flying Large Aircraft

Some players experience crashes when flying big aircraft (e.g., Airbus A330-743 Beluga XL, Airbus A400M, Boeing 747-8) near major airports like KLAX, LFPG, and KJFK.

✅ **Status: A fix is in progress.**

- Freelook Sensitivity (Mouse Control on Xbox)
- Freelook mode mouse movement may be too fast to keep under control.

✅ **Status: Investigation in Progress.**

- Game Freezes After Opening of Xbox Guide On "Ready To Fly" Screen. Some players find themselves unable to escape the game's frozen state if they open up the Xbox guide either during the flight or in the "Ready to Fly" screen.

✔️ Workaround: Press A to continue play, press Menu, then select Resume, and your controls will be back to normal.

COMMON ISSUES & FIXES

Missing Additional Content (Premium/Deluxe Versions)

If you've purchased an edition above Standard, there could be missing content on initial launch.

✔️ Fix: Simply restart the game and your content should be visible.

DX12 Error Message (Radeon RX580 or Older GPUs) If you have a DX12 error and your graphics card is Radeon RX580 or older, then the system does not have enough performance to run at that level.

✔️ Solution: This issue is fixed by getting a more powerful graphics card.

Crashes on CPUs with Over 32 Cores

If you are using a high-core-count CPU, e.g., Threadripper, Xeon, or top-of-the-line Ryzen processors, then the game will crash when launched.

✔️ Solution: Temporarily disable extra cores, keeping the active count to 32 or lower.

Can't Type Login Information at Startup

If you can't type in your login information when launching for the first time, the problem might be due to USB conflicts.

✔️ Solution: Disconnect all your USB peripherals except your mouse and keyboard, log in, then reconnect your peripherals.

Stuck on Loading After Logging in Xbox (PC)

If the game gets stuck after you've entered your Xbox login credentials:

✔️ Solution: Make sure your date and time settings are in the default Windows format.

Loading Problems (Game Freezes at 97%-98% or Random Errors)

If you become stuck at 97% or 98% during the loading screen:

✅ **Fix 1: Align your Time and Region Settings:**

1. Tap Settings > Date & Time

2. Set "Set time automatically" and "Set time zone automatically" ON

3. Tap on "Synchronize your clock"

4. Check your Region properly (e.g., Canada or USA mix-up)

✅ Fix 2: Move your installation folder to the C:\\\ drive if installed somewhere else. This solved the issue for some users as per their feedback.

✅ Fix 3: If your Windows user profile contains non-English characters such as "š" "ć" "\" try removing special characters from your certificate settings.

Google Mod Conflict (From MSFS 2020)

If you already had the Google Maps Mod installed in MSFS 2020, it could very well interfere with MSFS 2024.

✅ How to Repair It:

1. Open Notepad in Administrator Mode

2. Go to File > Open and navigate to:

C:\\Windows\\System32\\drivers\\etc

3. Open the host's file

4. Delete the following lines if they exist:

```

127.0.0.1 kh.ssl.ak.tiles.virtualearth.net

  127.0.0.1 khstorelive.azureedge.net

```

5. Save and exit

⚠️ Important Note: We do not recommend using any mod that substitutes Bing Maps with streamed third-party map data since other compatibility issues may be introduced.

fixing those issues, and thank you for your patience! Stay tuned for announcements as we keep working to improve the MSFS 2024 experience.

CHAPTER 6

MULTIPLAYER AND ONLINE EXPERIENCE

It's easy to see why so many aviation enthusiasts are hooked on Microsoft Flight Simulator 2024. From its jaw-dropping, photo-realistic landscapes to the intricate cockpit controls, it sets the gold standard for flight simulation. But what if you're craving something different? Maybe intense dogfights, fictional worlds, or full VR immersion? No problem, there's an entire fleet of flight games beyond that one with the potential to take such piloting adventures to new levels of greatness in all sorts of new and interesting ways.

Navigating into the Horizons of Microsoft Flight Simulator 2024

Whether you're looking for the thrill of air-to-air combat or simply enjoy the rush of arcade flight, there's an experience for every kind of pilot. What follows is a guide to flight simulators that take what makes Microsoft Flight Simulator 2024 exceptional but put their own spin on it.

1. X-Plane 12

- Platform: PC |
- Released: September 16, 2022 |
- Developer: Laminar Research

If realism is your cup of tea with Microsoft Flight Simulator 2024, then X-Plane 12 is the one you should be waiting for. Both simulators focus on realistic flight physics, so aircraft behave just like they do in real life, considering turbulence, weather, and aerodynamic forces. The game also features a variety of aircraft, from small private planes to massive commercial airliners, so you can experience everything from short flights to long-distance flights.

2. Digital Combat Simulator (DCS) World

DCS World is a serious war combat flight-simulation game for people interested in war, ranging from the Second World War to the modern era. Targeting using radar, weapon systems, and tactical dogfighting are just some of the things that one will find in this combat aviation simulation video game. While Microsoft Flight Simulator 2024 does have that open-world kind of scenario with civilian flight in a real manner, DCS World is more of a battlefield simulation environment with highly detailed aircraft and tactical warfare.

3. War Thunder

Platforms: PS4, PS5, Xbox One, Xbox Series X/S, PC | Developer: Gaijin Entertainment | ⚔ Multiplayer: Online

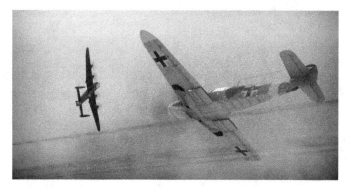

War Thunder is able to meld air, land, and sea combat together and make it work somehow fairly well, though it is fairly more action-oriented. Still impressive

nonetheless, however, for the actual physics of airplanes in the game and also extremely highly detailed airplane models. Unlike the very realistic civilian flying of Microsoft Flight Simulator 2024, War Thunder just puts people right in the midst of hot multiplayer dogfighting.

4. Aerofly FS 2 Flight Simulator

Aerofly FS 2 is not going to have as extensive global scenery as Microsoft Flight Simulator 2024, but it's a hugely detailed flier in itself. With Cessnas, Boeing 747s, and fully interactive 3D cockpits, it's a thoroughly immersive way of flying, especially over areas like the southwestern United States, where its scenery is most detailed.

5. GeoFS

If you're looking for a flight sim that runs on almost anything—including Chromebooks and smartphones—GeoFS is a surprisingly solid choice. While it can't match the realism of Microsoft Flight Simulator 2024, it provides a fun and accessible flying experience with over 30 aircraft, from planes and helicopters to hot air balloons.

6. VTOL VR

If you've ever fantasized about reaching out and flipping switches yourself in a fighter plane, then VTOL VR is the game for you. Designed from scratch for virtual reality, this game puts you right down in the cockpit, where you can work controls in a very hands-on way. From screaming dogfights to carrier landings, VTOL VR provides an immersion that flight simulators simply can't even aspire to come close to.

7. IL-2 Sturmovik: Battle of Stalingrad

For lovers of historically realistic flight battle simulations, IL-2 Sturmovik is a pleasure to indulge in. Set on the World War II Eastern Front, it has highly modeled planes with realistic damage and an "Expert Mode" for dedicated pilots who want realistic-to-the-point-of-scariness realism.

8. Project Wingman

If you want high-speed, action-packed dogfighting, Project Wingman is the game for you. Combining arcade flight with semi-realistic flight simulation, you'll be piloting the story-based campaign through a sequence of environments from tropical paradises to volcanic wastelands. It's not quite as realistic as Microsoft Flight Simulator 2024, but it gets something else right: the exhilaration of high-speed air combat.

Microsoft Flight Simulator 2024 is the gold standard of civilian flight sim games, but if you are thinking of soaring high in another way-either combat in the military, VR excitement, or entertainment-based on the internet-these have a great deal to offer as well. Whether you want to be a pilot of any sort, there is a game in the pipeline ready for liftoff!

FLYING WITH FRIENDS AND ONLINE COMMUNITIES

Looking for a flying buddy in Microsoft Flight Simulator? Want to learn from an experienced simmer, teach others, or even earn money by passing on your knowledge? FlyBeside is the solution. The new platform has been designed to bring flight simulation enthusiasts together and make it easy to connect, learn, and fly together.

A Marketplace for Learning

FlyBeside is a web-based marketplace for buying and selling individual flight lessons. Anyone who enjoys flight simulation can provide their lessons and sell them; no piloting or teaching experience in the real world is required. It's a great way of improving your skills or sharing your knowledge with others.

Find Your Perfect Flying Partner

The greatest hassle with multiplayer flight simulation has always been hunting down airmen worthy enough to fly alongside. Instead of looking through social media groups and forums scattered across the internet, FlyBeside makes it refreshingly easy using its powerful search and filtering abilities. Find copilots, wingmen, or instructors of your interest and skill level in a snap.

More Than Just Lessons

FlyBeside also boasts features for extending group flights and shared cockpit adventures. The third-party application YourControls can be utilized by the pilots and enjoy a shared cockpit flight together in a matter of ease.

Text and voice chat is also provided on the platform to enable live conversations.

Core Features

✔ **Lessons Marketplace** – Sell or buy personalized one-to-one flight lessons

✔ **Multiplayer Matchmaking** – Join and meet up with other pilots who would like to fly

✔ **Flight Buddy Requests** – Request to fly together with special mission goals/prefs

✔ **Group Flight Scheduling** – Coordinate and schedule multiplayer flights

Additional Functionality

✔ **Shared Cockpit & Wingman Flights** – Fly in tandem, with full co-pilot features

✔ **Advanced Search & Filter Tools** – Quickly find the right pilots and lessons

✔ **Pilot Profiles & Ratings** – View levels of experience and rate lessons

✔ **Flight Route Maps** – Plan and map flight routes

✔ **Badges & XP** – Gain participation rewards

✔ **Follow Pilots** – Get real-time updates from your instructors or flying buddies

✔ **Notification System** – Get notified about new lessons, flights & updates.

✔ **Web & Windows App** – Access easily from any device

✔ **Dedicated Discord Server** – Become part of the FlyBeside community

Whether you want to improve at flying, need to share your knowledge, or just want to find a good co-pilot, FlyBeside will make it easier than ever to play Microsoft Flight Simulator with others.

LIVE EVENTS AND CHALLENGES

Well, Microsoft Flight Simulator 2024 Tech Preview is underway now, and you may already have started noticing new content popping up. If you are wondering how to get to it or what we can expect in this stage, here's a quick rundown. We also have some news of future live streams from Microsoft-let's begin!

How to Get Into the Technical Alpha

Microsoft is inviting players to sign up for the technical alpha, an initial testing phase during which most of its features are still being developed. In contrast to beta testing, which occurs when a game is near completion and mostly needs bug fixing, the alpha testing tests concentrated systems and mechanics with less content.

This is the announcement from Microsoft about the alpha:

Most of the data we need will be passively received through your participation in the technical alpha. Throughout the technical alpha, we'll be monitoring new online services' usage and health through telemetry. Remember, the technical alpha is not about listening to your comments on the overall design or collection of features for Microsoft Flight Simulator 2024, and the quantity of what's available will be limited.

In short, this too is a phase all about the back-end testing of items like streamable data, weather, and traffic simulation; not necessarily the game. You may get a glimpse of UI issues or the like, and graphical improvements, but that is not the intent of fine-tuning here yet.

Glitches, lost content, and bugs are to be expected-but don't read too much into it because this is just part of the larger picture. It will come together with the actual release, and trust me I will be reporting on it when the day arrives!

If you want to be a part of the technical alpha, you can find out more and register yourself

I myself will be keeping an eye on the final launch to see it all come to fruition!

Live Streams & Dev Updates

As much as, or as little as, you're jumping in at the alpha, there is a lot of new content being brought your way! Content makers, streamers, and even Microsoft's development team themselves will be posting intel through live streams and dev updates leading up to launch.

Stay tuned-we have a whole calendar of events lined up so that you don't miss a thing!

Upcoming Live Streams & Dev Talks

It's going to be a busy next few week, building up to Microsoft Flight Simulator 2024! Remember to mark October 16, 23, and 30 with three further ones in November.

That means, among major highlights, that the sessions are going to be dedicated to aircraft partners - creators of many of the planes featured in the sim; each one of such streams will have four developers: "from well-known teams like iniBuilds, BlueMesh, Carenado, GotFriends, Miltech, and several others".

On October 30, there will also be a special Marketplace discussion and a World Partners talk that would hopefully delve into the scenery and world-building of the sim. To find out more about these events, look at the October 10 development update!

CUSTOMIZING YOUR MULTIPLAYER SETTINGS

And wait no more-Microsoft Flight Simulator 2024 is here! Whether a veteran virtual pilot or just starting out, the launch of a new simulator is always eagerly awaited-and sometimes a little daunting. With new aircraft, improved graphics, and engaging Career Mode, there's a lot to take in. But as with any major release, there may be a few bumps in the road.

To get you off to a flying start, we've put together some of the most important tips below. Follow these to avoid some of the common launch-day problems and learn as much as you can from your first flights!

1. Be Patient – Launch Days Can Be Unpredictable

Day-one spills and thrills are always in the mix with some glitches, and such server overload, unexpected bugs, and performance problems aren't rare for so huge a first release as this. And MSFS 2024 makes considerable use of cloud computing-that is, online services will be in high demand when simmers all around the world take the plunge.

Our suggestion? Spend the first couple of days as a test run. Experiment with new features, familiarize yourself with updated systems, and avoid diving headfirst into complex add-ons. And expect patches and updates to begin flowing in prompt fashion, for which keep monitoring official channels for the latest enhancements and fixes.

2. Do Not Overfill the Community Folder

One of the worst things you can do on launch day is to dump all your old MSFS 2020 add-ons into MSFS 2024. With the sim promoting a new engine, structural improvements, and a Career Mode, many of the older mods won't be compatible-and may even cause stability issues.

✔ **Start fresh**: Get the simulator up and running in its vanilla form first.

Checklist the following to do this:

✔ Do a test before adding any third-party content.

✔ Reintroduce add-ons one by one to see if they're working as expected.

Go slowly, as one outdated mod can just make a random crash or performance loss.

3. Re-Configure Your Controls From Scratch

If you are upgrading from MSFS 2020, here is some important news: your previously set control profiles will not be migrated, so you will need to manually reconfigure your yoke, joystick, throttle quadrant, or gamepad all over again. Since MSFS 2024 will include new aircraft with some career-related interactions, it is perhaps nice to assign some keys yourself for firefighting equipment, cargo activities, and newer avionics systems.

✔ Test all your peripherals so they can be sure that they were recognized.

✔ Customize controls for airliners, general aviation planes, helicopters, hot air balloons, etc.

✔ Save multiple profiles so you can fly using different flying styles. And remember, a few minutes now will save headaches later!

4. Optimize Graphics for Smooth Performance

MSFS 2024 is gorgeous, but the more detailed graphics, the lighting effects, and the verdant biomes all require plenty of juice as well. Optimized to perform as well as MSFS 2020, it's probably not a great plan to just turn everything up to ultra-settings immediately.

✔ The best place to start is with the medium-to-high settings and see from there.

✔ Be aware of photogrammetry-dense regions and weather that demands even more processing power.

✔ Turn some settings back when needed to provide room for framerate over maxed-out settings to keep the simulator smooth.

And don't forget to update your graphics drivers before launching the sim!

5. Dive into Career Mode; Try New Aircraft

One of the cool things about MSFS 2024 is a feature called Career Mode, which adds a new layer of realism and challenge. You can:

- Aerial firefighter – Combat wildfires from the air.
- Air ambulance pilot – Flying medical emergency missions.
- Cargo hauler – Hauling freight between different areas.

With the widest range of aircraft of any MSFS release, there's something for everyone-from hot air balloons to next-generation electric planes, this is your chance to break out of that comfort zone and try something totally new!

6. Enjoy the Scenery – Go Bush Flying!

More diverse biomes, terrain textures, and seasonal effects-the reason why MSFS 2024 is every bush pilot's and VFR flyer's wet dream. Some to look out for are:

- The Grand Canyon
- Alaska's backcountry airstrips
- Scenic spots in North America and Europe

Low and slow flight will give you the real chance to observe the improved terrain details and realistic light effects. If you fly airliners, you will be also able to observe this on cityscapes and big airports.

7. Be part of the MSFS Community

Microsoft has gone out loud and clear that MSFS 2024 was "built for the community, with the community." Whether via multiplayer events, forums, or even just Discord groups, the experience is even more refined by being part of the flight sim community.

✔ Subscribe to YouTube channels and livestreams for tutorials and tips.

✔ Share experiences through forums and social media groups.

✔ Learn from fellow pilots and discover new challenges together.

The launch of Microsoft Flight Simulator 2024 is just the beginning! By taking a patient, gradual approach, optimizing your settings, and embracing the community, you'll set yourself up for countless hours of immersive flying.

CHAPTER 7

CONSTRUCTING FLIGHT PLANS AND REALISTIC NAVIGATION

Flight simulation isn't gazing into another world to decide if things work or don't but rather an appreciation of systems, tools, and procedures where, yes, aviation does work.

Tom Carroll has been a name to trust within the MSFS community for many years with his comprehensive guides that fill the gap between enjoyable flying and realistic simulation. His new book, MSFS 2024 Navigation and Flight Planning, goes in-depth into modern navigation and deciphers the latest breakthroughs in MSFS 2024.

The previous e-Books written by Carroll are now quick-paced resources that simmer simmers to get depth and clarity. They are:

- MSFS Next Level: Missed Approaches & Holds, 2021
- MSFS Next Level: A Practical Guide to the CJ4, 2021
- MSFS Next Level: Old School, 2022
- MSFS Next Level: Realism, 2024

What distinguishes Carroll's guides from others is the fact that they are so easily readable. He is really adept at dissecting challenging aviation theories in a fashion that is well understood by pilots of all types. His latest book is consistent with this precedent, describing MSFS 2024's changes while reestablishing basic principles of navigation.

In a world of YouTube guides and forum discussion, Carroll's eBooks are different: structured, reliable content that a simmer can refer to at any time. They provide you with:

- Comprehensive Learning-Workflow-by-workflow instead of stand-alone tips.
- Visual Guidance-More than 270 images in the new book.
- Long-Term Value-A reference to return to mid-air during the flight or during practice sessions.

Carroll's book remains the go-to handbook for anyone seriously interested in learning the navigation and flight planning aspect of MSFS 2024.

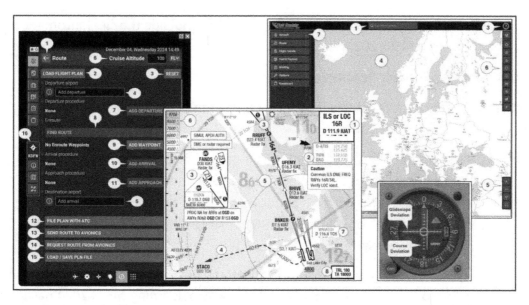

MSFS 2024 Navigation and Flight Planning

For just $9, this 154-page eBook is all about all you've ever wanted to know regarding flying and navigating in Microsoft Flight Simulator 2024.

Part 1: Mastering Navigation Fundamentals Techniques

First of all, Carroll describes the basics of aviation navigation, outlining classical and modern techniques:

- NDB Navigation — Applying skills to utilize older but highly applicable Non-Directional Beacons.
- VOR/ILS Approaches — Radials and Instrument Landing System aligning.
- GPS & RNAV — Leverage of contemporary workflows, including LPV precision approaches.

Part 2: Uncovering MSFS 2024

The guide then addresses the new functionality added in MSFS 2024 and describes how to use the new in-game flight planning system:

- World Map Interface – How to use this brand-new interface for route planning, aircraft configuration, and weather management.
- Electronic Flight Bag (EFB) – In-sim assets for navigation, performance calculation, and checklists.

- Web Flight Planner - Allow routes to be planned outside the sim, automatically syncing in to MSFS 2024.

Part 3: Practical Flight Scenarios

The theory is demonstrated in the below four hands-on flight exercises with instructor guidance to implement basic concepts, which are:

- **NDB Navigation** - Raw Data flight, making an NDB approach.
- **VOR Tracking -** Flying radials to navigate, featuring a VOR approach.
- **GPS/RNAV Approach**: Perform an RNAV/LPV precision landing.
- **Hybrid Navigation:** Combined VOR, RNAV, and ILS procedures for easy mode switching between systems.

More than 270 screenshots, such as cockpit shots and highlighted charts, are contained within this guide to provide an orderly, in-the-sim way of learning MSFS 2024 navigation systems.

A long-awaited in-depth study-level book, MSFS 2024 Navigation and Flight Planning, authored by Tom Carroll is now available at his website for just $9 USD.

GENERATING PRECISE FLIGHT ROUTES

Flight planning is the mapping of the safe and efficient route of an aircraft from departure to destination. Since there could be thousands of aircraft in the air at any given time, careful planning ensures smooth flight operations, adherence to ATC, and reduces the risk of mid-air collision. Flight planning also considers whether an aircraft would be capable of taking off safely and reaching particular airports safely under both regulations and conditions.

Electronic Flight Bags: The New Way of Flight Planning

Manual paper calculations are a thing of the past—pilots nowadays utilize Electronic Flight Bags to plan flights and calculate aircraft performance. Such electronic devices streamline the process by automatically incorporating the following factors:

- Aircraft specifications
- Current weather conditions
- Airspace restrictions
- Runway data

These will be inclusive of:

- Atmospheric pressure and wind speed
- Aircraft weight and payload

All of these in computations made in real time mean a major improvement in efficiency and accuracy, and so EFBs are a critical utility in modern aviation.

What Constitutes a Flight Plan?

A flight plan is in formal structure, but the details will differ depending on the type of flight. Pilots may file under different categories, including:

- **VFR**: Visual Flight Rules, which are visual navigation by landmarks and air regulations.
- **IFR:** Instrument Flight Rules, utilizing navigation aids to assist in flying, normally when conditions are poor.
- **Composite Flight Plan (VFR + IFR):** When both visual and instrument navigation are employed.
- **Defense VFR Flight Plan (DVFR):** For defence or security flight.
- **International Flight Plan (IFP) -** Filed for crossing international borders.

COMPONENTS OF A FLIGHT PLAN

1. Departure and Arrival Airports

It begins with takeoff and landing site. This not only decides the route of flight but also the amount of fuel that the plane needs to carry. It also includes choosing an alternate airport in case weather or operational issues make it impossible to land at the planned destination. The conditions on the runway, runway length, and the facilities for the safe landing of the plane are taken into account.

2. Flight Path and Route Adjustments

The flight plan indicates the route along which the aircraft will fly from when it departs until when it arrives, crossing various checkpoints. Key among them are:

- Altitude
- Groundspeed and direction
- Vertical rate
- Estimated time over the route

Even though a course is charted prior to departure, heading, speed, and altitude can be changed by the pilot in flight to avoid adverse weather or air traffic buildup.

Apart from the above, in VFR flights, other elements that would be taken into account are:

- Airspace restrictions
- Geographical landmarks for navigation
- Visual references such as windsocks and runway lights
- Airplane capability and payload variation
- ICAO regulations

Regardless of the category in which one is to fly, VFR or IFR, a properly planned flight plan will make sure that the aforementioned flight is conducted efficiently, safely, and smoothly.

flight path in an electronic flight bag app

KEY FACTORS IN FLIGHT PLANNING: A PILOT'S GUIDE

Altitude: Finding a Happy Medium

How high an aircraft flies has important implications for both its fuel consumption and its flight time. Selecting the proper flight altitude is extremely critical to optimum fuel efficiency with safety of flight in weather conditions.

Fuel Efficiency & Planning: Get Every Drop

Flight planning is not just getting from one point to another but doing it in an efficient manner. Fuel burn optimization greatly benefits airlines and operators since fuel costs comprise a large part of the overall costs.

Fuel demands are influenced by a number of factors:

- Flight distance
- Aircraft consumption rate per flight, in relation to the payload
- Weather conditions en-route

There must be enough fuel on board, not merely to make the destination, but enough in case diversions become necessary.

Among the other significant influences, the jet stream forms intense currents of air moving through the Earth's atmosphere. These play important roles in a flight, as these winds can help or hinder an airplane. A typical example is travel between Europe and North America, where strong tailwinds shorten flying time and fuel use; travel into the jet stream for the return journey requires additional energy and fuel.

Weather: Planning for the Unpredictable

- Destination and route weather need to be carefully forecast before flying. Weather on long flights can change drastically, so pilots use several current reports and forecasts, including:
- METARs (current weather reports)
- TAFs (Terminal Aerodrome Forecasts)
- Radar imagery
- Wind forecasts
- SIGMETs and AIRMETs (hazard warnings for turbulence, storms, or icing)

Knowing what is happening outside, the pilot can plan for turbulence, visibility, or even runway conditions that could be a challenge.

Weight & Balance: Keeping It Safe and Stable

Sample of weight and balance calculations in a flight planning app

Aircraft weight balance is extremely important when it comes to flight safety. All planes are regulated through maximum permissible weight, and even in those weights the balance affects performance and stability. Some of the key points to consider are:

- Passengers and luggage weight
- Cargo distribution
- Fuel load
- Changes in center of gravity

Any change in cargo, fuel, or passengers requires recalculating weight and balance so the plane can be safely flown.

Communication: Coordinating for a Smooth Flight

A flight plan is not just about charts and numbers; it's also about communication. P мотивам from straightforward to complicated, depending on the flight, pilots need to communicate with:

- **Dispatchers**: route approval and fuel planning
- **Co-pilots and flight crews**: flight operations
- **Air Traffic Control (ATC)** (in terms of ground clearance and route change in real-time)
- **Modern Electronic Flight Bags (EFBs)**: support communication through integration of flight information, sending reports via email, and posting on cloud networks to enable convenient collaboration.

Emergency Procedures: Ready for the Unforeseen

Flight crew must be adequately trained on emergency procedures; these are:

- Engine failure procedure-engine out procedures, EOP
- In-flight emergency management
- Emergency landing and ditching procedures

Every airport has its emergency parameters: safe altitudes and planned vectors to take in the event of an unforeseen event. Adequate planning along with proper training ensures a prompt and correct response if necessary.

Altitude Selection, Fuel Efficiency, Weather Forecasting, Weight Management, Communication, and Emergency Preparedness-all these are utilized to ensure a safer, more efficient flight.

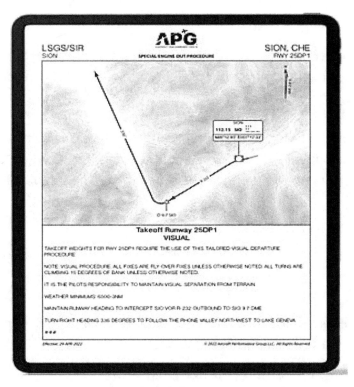

Example Engine Out Procedure (EOP) for KASE airport in Aspen, Colorado

Filing a Flight Plan: An Easy and Quick Guide

Filing a flight plan is a crucial step in ensuring a safe and well-coordinated flight. It officially documents your planned route, confirms that you've checked weather conditions and airspace restrictions, and notifies the Federal Aviation Administration (FAA) of your intended path.

Before filing, you'll need some key details, including:

- Aircraft type
- True airspeed
- Tail number

It is also noteworthy that the FAA has mandated the filing of most flight plans using the International Civil Aviation Organization's ICAO format for standardized filings. Filings may be made domestically, however, on flights not subject to the requirements of ICAO. In fact, this domestic system will be eventually phased out.

Means of Filing a Flight Plan

For convenience, whether you prefer a new, all-electronic means of filing your flight plan or an archaic paper method is your preference. Some options include the following:

1. Flight Planning Apps: The Quickest

Tablet and smartphone-based flight planning software saves pilots' time - only a few minutes to file. All apps will include aircraft data pre-entered into them that will automatically calculate performance. In addition to filing, the software includes access to:

- Chart data and runway analysis
- Weight and balance tools
- Engine-out procedures
- Geo-referenced plates

Software such as iPreFlight Genesis PRO also facilitates easy sharing of plans with dispatchers, flight crews, and air traffic controllers.

2. Filing by Phone: The Conventional Technique

If you want to do things a little more manually, you can also file a flight plan by phone at 1-800-WX-BRIEF (1-800-922-7433). Just let the briefer know where you're flying out of and give them your flight details. The briefer will read back to you to confirm and then confirm the filing.

3. Filing Online: Quick and Convenient

The pilots could also submit flight plans through 1800wxbrief.com, the FAA's official website for ICAO and domestic flight plan submission. You can log in and thus save a list of common travel routes; this will help you more with saving time while submitting and, thus, saving even more time for preparing for takeoff.

Whatever of these techniques one uses, the flight plan is documented and accessible to the appropriate aviation authorities, significantly easing and making your flight more secure. Learning air traffic control and communication

Adding Some Realism to Your Flight Sim with ATC

If you want your flight simulator experience to be even better, then incorporating ATC is what you need. If you are flying using Microsoft Flight Simulator (MSFS), X-Plane, or

Prepar3D, adding ATC simply makes flights so much more realistic, interactive, and engaging.

Let us dissect and see why ATC is a must-have in your sim, and most importantly, who are the power players.

Why Use ATC in Your Flight Sim?

1. Feels Like the Real Thing

ATC in the real-world coordinate's aircraft movement, minimizing the risk of flights and making them more effective. The air is not void-thousands of flights are airborne at any moment. If you include ATC in your simulator, then you will feel like airspace coordination and make flying more realistic and interactive.

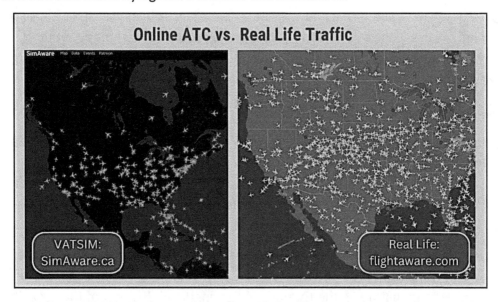

VATSIM is a popular online Air Traffic Control network

2. It Makes Flights More Interactive

Solo flying in a simulator is somewhat lonely, but with ATC, you're directly in a living, multiplayer world. Use the 2023 Navigraph Community Survey, for example. It found that almost 48% of simmers have flown online with ATC over the past year. That's correct; you become a part of an active community of controllers and pilots!

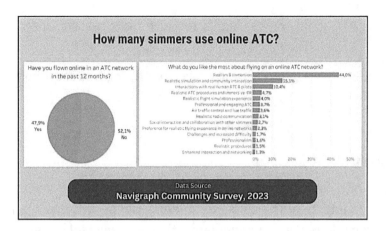

Data Source
Navigraph Community Survey, 2023

3. It's Challenging and Rewarding

At first, studying ATC communications takes a newfound skill and sense of excitement to your flying. Precise, concise instructions delivered, proper "phraseology" utilized, and answering correctly in dense airspace has you feeling like a real pilot. After getting good at it, it's flat-out habit-forming!

4. It Can Even Save You Money

For student pilots, practice in a simulator with ATC builds confidence prior to getting into a live cockpit. Most state that this reduced their degree of out-of-the-box nervousness when actually communicating with real controllers. By practicing from home, you can gain more flying time in the air focusing on flight rather than messing around with radio calls, which can pay for itself in training expenses.

"Flying with VR in MSFS on VATSIM totally transformed my flight sim universe. Being an eternally student pilot, it provided me with the next best thing to piloting the real aircraft. Other than, naturally, the thunder of the engine and aroma of the avgas!"

— Howard Rhett, Student Pilot

ATC OPTIONS: HUMAN VS. AUTOMATED

For flight simulator ATC, you have two major options:

- Live human controllers (for maximum realism)
- Automated ATC systems (for a more relaxed, offline experience)

Let's examine both.

Option 1: Online Networks (Human Controllers)

Real-time ATC networks literally connect you with actual human beings acting as controllers, just like aviation in the real world. Some of the most popular platforms are:

☑ **VATSIM** – A large network composed entirely of volunteers with controllers literally all across the globe.

☑ **IVAO** – Very much like VATSIM, placing even greater emphasis on training and realism.

☑ **PilotEdge** – Paid-for service with pro controllers; sometimes used for training actual pilots.

With these networks, you'll experience:

✔ Real-time controller instructions

✔ Authentic aviation phraseology

✔ Unexpected changes (like last-minute runway shifts)

✔ A thriving community of aviation enthusiasts

Option 2: Automated ATC Systems

If you're new to ATC or prefer a solo experience, automated ATC may be a better fit.

Incorated Sim ATC: MSFS and X-Plane have in incorporated ATC out of the box but very simplistic.

Third-Party Add-on programs: Applications such as Pilot2ATC and PF3 ATC offer Voice recognition among many more realistic interactions of actual ATC.

Automated ATC will never come anywhere close to being as unpredictable to work with as human controllers but is a wonderfully low-stress method of learning basic interactions without having to deal with actual human controllers.

The Best Online ATC Networks

It's time to get down deep on some of the best human-controlled ATC networks:

PilotEdge – The Gold Standard for Realism

What makes it so unique?

- Pro-grade ATC used by actual flight schools
- Western U.S. coverage assured with controllers

- Great resource for serious training or student pilots
- Compatible with MSFS, X-Plane and P3D
- Subscription begins at $19.95/month (as of Jan 2025), with a free trial offered
- VATSIM – The Most Popular Free Option

VATSIM is a giant online ATC network with controllers all over the world who donate their time for free. Want to try for free to have real human ATC? Look no further.

✅ **Major airspaces' live controllers**

Thousands of active pilots at a single-time Compliant with MSFS, X-Plane, and P3D Absolutely free to use

Which ATC Option is Right for You?

- Want a pro-level experience? → PilotEdge is the ticket.
- Need free live ATC? → Try VATSIM or IVAO.
- Like to practice offline? → Use built-in sim ATC or an AI-based add-on.

Either of those will transport you, with the addition of ATC, from solo flying in your simulator to a fully interactive realistic experience.

If you fly flight sims looking for an extra degree of realism in the skies, here is a list of virtual networks committed to pairing pilots and controllers from all over the world.

VATSIM – Community-Driven Free ATC Network

VATSIM Virtual Air Traffic Simulation Network: arguably the most important website for online, community-based ATC among sim pilots currently. This software links your simulator to live controllers as volunteers and other pilots, hence offering truly immersive real-time flights.

X-plane, MSFS, P3D compatibility

best for IFR flight, mostly airliner operation

☑ ATC Quality Varies, since controllers are volunteers

☑ Cost Completely free!

While VATSIM is a great experience, it does not offer professional ATC at all times, unlike pay services like PilotEdge.

IVAO – Another Free ATC Network

IVAO, or International Virtual Aviation Organization, offers similar experiences to that of VATSIM, offering worldwide ATC coverage with its client software.

☑ Stronger presence in some areas where VATSIM has fewer controllers, particularly in parts of Europe, Asia, and South America

☑ Also free with a thriving community

Getting Started with VATSIM or IVAO

To join these networks, you'll need:

✔ A supported flight simulator (X-Plane, MSFS, or P3D)

✔ A stable internet connection

✅ A headset with microphone for voice chat text chat can be used too, but is not recommended)

✅ The network client software used by question VATSIM uses vPilot, IVAO uses IvAp

Flying Online with ATC Tips

- Do not spawn on the runway immediately always spawn at a gate or parking
- Check which controllers are online prior to starting your flight
- Fly during less busy hours (early mornings are usually quieter)

✍️ Keep a pen and paper handy for taxi routes and clearances

Automated ATC Options for Any Flight Simulator

If you'd rather fly without relying on live controllers, several add-ons provide AI-powered or automated ATC services.

Pilot2ATC

A complete ATC add-on for MSFS, FSX, P3D, and X-Plane supporting IFR as well as VFR flights.

- Speech communication with voice recognition
- Text-based user interface for typed people
- 10-day free trial available to drive it around ⏸️⏸️
- Inbuilt and Add-on ATC for Microsoft Flight Simulator (MSFS)

MSFS Inbuilt ATC

MSFS has a very simple ATC system with voice interaction by menu choice.

✅ Simple to use to get people off the ground - literally

Warning Not for actual real-world pilot training as it uses incorrect phraseology

FSHud (For IFR Flying Only)

This ATC addon improves IFR flying with:

- Several voices generated with AI
- Full integration of SimBrief & Navigraph
- **X Radio**: Provides multi radio feature to receive multiple frequencies at the same time.

ProATC/SR (Speech Recognition)

ProATC/X covers all IFR Flights in MSFS, P3D and FSX providing voice communication method both ways with Global ATC Coverage.

FOR X-PLANE - ATC OPTIONS

Integrated ATC X-Plane12

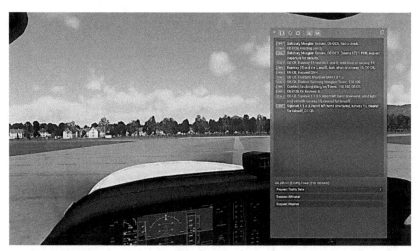

X-plane has continued development on its internally available ATC to offer for IFR, much better but still not optimal coverage for both VFR operations.

X-ATC Chatter

- Plays real ATC recordings from over 45,000 clips collected via LiveATC.net
- Not interactive—it enhances immersion but doesn't let you talk to controllers
- Offers a free demo

AI-Powered ATC Solutions (Next-Gen ATC for Sim Pilots)

BeyondATC

Released in May 2024, BeyondATC is one of the most advanced AI-driven ATC solutions for MSFS.

- More than 350+ regional AI voices
- IFR support with realistic routing
- FAA & ICAO phraseology created with real controllers
- Real-time traffic injection for realistic aircraft behaviour

But that's not all. Further updates will include:

✈️ VFR support

- Emergency procedures
- Oceanic operations

SayIntentions.ai

Another AI-based ATC software for MSFS & X-Plane. It supports:

☑ Voice Recognition & Natural Language Processing

☑ Dynamic Routing & Real-Time Weather Integration

☑ Multiple Languages Support

The Bottom Line: AI-based ATC is a great option to learn good radio communication without needing live human controllers, yet AI has not yet achieved human ATC networks' capabilities.

BECOMING A VIRTUAL AIR TRAFFIC CONTROLLER

If you ever want to know who is on the other side of the radio, well, virtual air traffic controlling may be an incredibly fascinating experience that you could be a part of. VATSIM, IVAO, and PilotEdge all have a training program for getting you on it. It's an excellent way of learning ATC procedure, but you'll also learn to be a better pilot.

Choosing the Right ATC Option for You

These are just a few of your choices, how would you select the best to meet your requirement?

1. Know Your Comfort Level

Nervous microphone speaking: Simply tune in on LiveATC.net, say, and listen to the live ATC. You learn a lot by osmosis this way. Or find an automated ATC plugin through which you can pause mid-scene as you please, something you can't do with live networks such as VATSIM.

If you are comfortable speaking or are a student pilot: Begin with live ATC networks. These are facilities like VATSIM, IVAO, or PilotEdge. If you are training in the real world, live ATC is invaluable since you shouldn't learn any bad habits picked up from automated systems that won't necessarily hold up to the procedures for your airspace.

2. Evaluate Flying Skills

- Beginners: Stick to automated ATC until comfortable with the basic flying.
- More experienced pilots: The live networks have realistic challenge and are a great opportunity to keep sharp with your communications.

3. What Type of Flying Do You Do?

For VFR pilots: PilotEdge is perfect, especially for flight students in the real world. Automated ATC misses VFR subtleties that are based on airspace class (Class B, C, D, etc.). - For IFR and Airline ops: VATSIM and IVAO are perfect to operate airlines and IFR with a large userbase and routes to mix it up.

4. Search for Regional Coverage

If you are a real-world pilot, you'll want to choose a network that most closely serves your local procedures. While general aviation procedures are similar all around the world, there do exist some variations country to country.

PilotEdge only handles the western U.S., so if you like to practice flying out of an East Coast airport VATSIM might be the ticket.

Keep in mind that VATSIM is not always supported by ATC when you want to fly, so you may have to make some compromises.

5. Timing is everything

PilotEdge operates on a set schedule of 8 AM – 11 PM Pacific. If that does not mesh with your own schedule, you might consider searching elsewhere.

VATSIM and IVAO are both volunteer-operated, so controllers are more active during evenings and weekends of their respective timezones.

6. Community & Events

If you like community flying, VATSIM and IVAO both organize events where you can fly in high-density airspaces with live ATC.

Learning ATC: A New Skill to Master

Talking to ATC in a flight simulator is just like learning any new language; it requires patience, time, and a sense of being able to soak up a couple of mistakes.

Tips for Success

Embrace the learning curve: Don't worry too much about making mistakes; remember that controllers have been applied to communicating with all types of pilots on live networks.

Listen often: While driving to and from work or running errands, listen to real-world ATC communication via LiveATC.net. It is a way to learn by osmosis.

Free training courses: VATSIM and PilotEdge offer formal course instruction. As an example, PilotEdge has VFR (CAT ratings) and IFR (I-ratings) course instruction.

NEED EXTRA HELP?

1-on-1 coaching -Your flight instructor can be an ATC controller. They help you practice in a no or very low-pressure environment. Flight Sim Coach provides one-on-one private coaching on VFR and IFR communications.

Recommended reading-AIM by FAA is an excellent free resource; Pilot's Handbook of Aeronautical Knowledge by the FAA, 'Say Again, please' by Bob Gardner, is also a nice good, easy read.

Training apps – The PlaneEnglish ARSim app is an interactive method of practicing ATC comms without the expense of a full flight sim.

Throwing some ATC into your flight sim makes it all so much more realistic. Live networks are, of course, the most realistic experience, but employing automated ATC or passive listening is an excellent way to gain confidence.

Find out what suits you best, and should you need any help, Flight Sim Coach is here for you:

✔ Sim configuration & ATC add-on installation

✔ Tailor-made coaching to learn exceptional ATC communications

Here's to crossing paths in the virtual skies! ✈

CHAPTER 8

INSTALLING ADD-ONS AND THIRD-PARTY MODS

Mods are community-created tweaks that build on and enrich your Microsoft Flight Simulator experience. Mods can stretch from upgrading visuals, introducing new aircraft, tweaking physics, to adding entirely new elements to the sim.

How to Install Mods

In order to install a mod, place its files inside the Community folder.

Here's where to look for the Community folder depending on your installation type:

Microsoft Store/Xbox App:

`C:\Users\YourUsername\AppData\Local\Packages\Microsoft.FlightSimulator_8wekyb3d8bbwe\LocalCache\Packages\Community`

Steam Version:

`C:\Users\YourUsername\AppData\Roaming\Microsoft Flight Simulator\Packages\Community`

Tip: Windows 10 and 11 hide the AppData folder by default. To reveal it, open File Explorer, click on the View tab, and check Hidden items.

TROUBLESHOOTING: MOD NOT VISIBLE IN THE SIM

If your mod is not showing up in the simulator, check installation:

1. Open the Community folder and locate your mod.

2. Inside the mod folder, place the files manifest.json and layout.json at the root.

If all is installed properly and the mod still won't load, attempt to restart the simulator or check that the mod is working with your existing version of the game.

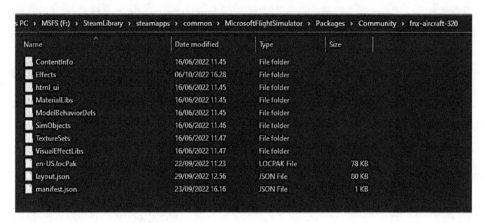

If your mod isn't showing up in Microsoft Flight Simulator, then it may be installed into the wrong Community folder; this can happen if you've chosen to install to a custom path. You'd have two Community folders in this case: one in your selected custom install path and one under C:\\Users\\YourUsername\\AppData.

Finding the Correct Mod Folder

To check where the simulator is actually looking for mods:

1. Navigate to C:\\Users\\YourUsername\\AppData\\.

2. Look for the UserCfg.opt file.

3. Open it with Notepad and go to the bottom.

4. Find the line starting with InstalledPackagesPath.

Example:

This is the path that the simulator is looking for mods. If this is incorrect, you can do it by hand, save the file, and then reboot the sim.

Can't Find the "Community" Folder?

If you simply can't find your community folder at all, try the following:

1. Open Microsoft Flight Simulator.

2. Go to Options > General Options > Developers and switch ON Developer Mode. done

3. Open Developer Toolbar then Tools > Virtual File System > Packages Folders. done

4. Press Open Community Folder.

This will have you right in the folder the sim is referencing for mods and that path should match what's in your UserCfg.opt file.

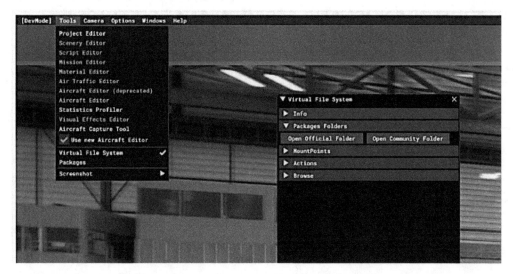

Some mods have additional setup procedures. Always follow the instructions from the mod creator to guarantee correct installation.

⚠ Important Warnings

Mods are not Microsoft Flight Simulator official products, so remember these facts before using them:

USE AT YOUR OWN RISK - Mods can impact Windows 10/11 device stability and security.

NOT SUPPORTED BY MICROSOFT - The Flight Simulator team does not own, test or administer mods, and therefore can't guarantee performance or debug.

Possible compatibility issues — A future update of the simulator could render the use of mods invalid. Uninstall the mods first before updating to avoid issues; see How to Install a New Update Safely.

Achievements and some of the game features may not work with mods enabled.

Privacy concerns — Some mods can access your Xbox Live and device data, which could be hacked.

No official content rating: Mods are neither rated by the ESRB nor other regulatory boards and may contain unsuitable content for all.

Always be careful and download mods from safe websites!

ADJUSTING GRAPHICS AND PERFORMANCE SETTINGS

If you experience serious performance issues with MSFS, this is what you must do to get your computer running MSFS as smoothly as can be.

1 Check System Requirements

Begin by making sure your PC is fulfilling the system requirements:

- If your system barely meets the minimum requirements– It will function but you may experience performance losses unless you turn down the graphical settings.
- If your machine is up to the recommended specs– You should have a smoother game, though the most demanding settings will be extremely taxing.

2 Keep Your System Updated

Ensure Windows 10/11 is updated. If needed, refer to Windows troubleshoot resources for help.

3 Disable CPU & GPU Overclocking

Overclocking can cause heatup and hardware degradation in the long term. If your machine is overclocked:

- Disable Intel SpeedStep within your BIOS settings.
- Decrease or turn off CPU overclock values.
- Turn off GPU overclocking, user custom settings, within Radeon Software or Nvidia nTune.
- Use your manufacturer's documentation for recommendations.

4 Turn Off Hardware-Accelerated GPU Scheduling

This option occasionally may lead to worse performance.

1. Open Settings → System → Display → Graphics Settings

2. Turn Hardware-accelerated GPU scheduling OFF

3. Restart your PC.

5 Clean Install GPU Drivers Your older or corrupted GPU drivers could be to blame.

How to update them the right way:

1. Windows Key → type "Add or Remove Programs"

2. Uninstall your current graphics driver

3. Restart your computer

4. Download and install the new driver:

- Nvidia: [Get latest drivers] (https://www.nvidia.com/)
- AMD: [Get latest drivers] (https://www.amd.com/)

5. Reboot once more after installation.

6. Use the Dedicated GPU

In case your PC has both integrated graphics and a dedicated GPU, ensure MSFS utilizes the dedicated one.

For Nvidia: Navigate to Nvidia Control Panel → 3D Settings → Manage 3D Settings → Under "Program Settings," click MSFS to select it. Move it under High Performance Nvidia Processor.

Open Radeon Setting → under Preference, Additional Settings-Power-Switchable Graphics Application Settings under MSFS → High performance.

7 Disabled Full-Screen Optimizations

In case you have a non-100% DPI on your screen, it may cause a problem.

- FlightSimulator.exe
- Right-click → Properties → Compatibility
- Click Change high DPI settings
- Set "Override high DPI scaling behavior" and to Application

8 Adapt Nvidia GeForce Experience Settings

Nvidia GeForce Experience will be set to optimize the game by default - which is not always the best.

1. Open GeForce Experience

2. Go to Games & Apps

3. uncheck "Automatically optimize newly added games"

9. Close Background Apps & Overlays

Discord, Nvidia Shadowplay, Xbox Game Bar and other background programs are overlays and will slow MSFS down. Switch them off periodically as they will likely become active again via updates.

Some common ones to turn off:

- AMD Radeon ReLive
- Discord Overlay
- Nvidia Shadowplay
- Razer Cortex Gamecaster
- Twitch Overlay

Clear DirectX Shader Cache

Stuttering typically is resolved after shader cache clearing:

1. Open Disk Cleanup

2. Select your MSFS Installation Drive

3. Mark only DirectX Shader Cache, do not check anything else (make the other boxes blank unless you absolutely want to clear their content as well)

4. Hit OK

Adjust GPU Cache Allocation

Certain GPUs offer you control over shader cache settings for performance optimization.

For Nvidia: Open Nvidia Control Panel → 3D Settings > Shader Cache Setting → Increase the cache value.

For AMD: Change cache tuning settings via Radeon Software.

Check your GPU's manual to find out what the best settings are.

Enable/Disable Game Mode

Windows Game Mode can be enabled in order to maximize gaming performance. Try turning it on/off and see what holds:

1. Open Settings → Gaming

2. Go to Game Mode

3. Turn Game Mode ON (or OFF) and check.

Increase Virtual Memory (Pagefile Size)

Increasing virtual memory helps if your system has less RAM.

1. In the Windows search, enter "Advanced System Settings".

2. In the Advanced tab, under Performance, click Settings.

3. Again in Advanced tab → Virtual Memory → Change.

4. Uncheck "Automatically manage paging file size."

5. Choose the drive where Windows is installed-mostly C:.

6. Assign a custom pagefile size according to your RAM (recommendations: 1.5x to 2x of your total RAM).

7. Click Set → OK → Restart your PC.

Power Settings & Disable Power Monitoring Apps

Windows might throttle performance in order to save power.

Open Settings → System → Power & battery → Screen and sleep.

- Click Additional Power Settings → Switch to High Performance mode.
- Shut down your PC completely (not restart).

Disable any Power Monitoring Apps that may be running in the background and throttling performance; these include:

- MSI DragonCenter
- RyzenMaster
- Dell Killer Control Center (Gamefast)

Graphics Settings Changes within MSFS

Changes in graphics settings from within the game:

1. Open Microsoft Flight Simulator

2. Go to Options → General Options → Graphics

3. Lower Render Scaling to 80 (instead of 100 or higher).

4. Under Advanced Settings, test FXAA instead of TAA.

5. Click Apply & Save (F11).

Experiment to find the best balance between performance and visuals.

Follow these steps so that you receive peak performance without stuttering, crashing, and slowing down halfway through in Microsoft Flight Simulator. 🛫

MSFS 2024 BEST GRAPHICS AND FPS SETTINGS

Microsoft Flight Simulator 2024 raises the stakes for flight simulation with its promises of enhanced graphics and greater immersion. With the power of advanced cloud computing and machine learning, tweaks from MSFS 2020 are poised to make the simulated world even more realistic. But as any serious simmer would know, finding that sweet spot between breathtaking visuals and flawless performance is easier said than done.

The multitude of options for graphics settings can perplex anyone in the process of figuring out where to go from here with such a setting and which would be best. Here comes Dwindling FPS to the rescue-a YouTube channel that helps by showing all settings one at a time with its implication so as to make your flight sim perfect and not overheat your PC to turn it into some sort of heater.

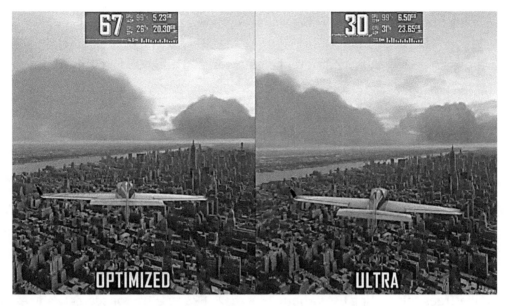

It goes through each of the graphics settings in MSFS 2024 one by one and shows the effect of each tweak on image quality and framerate. Some have a huge effect, others barely- except for how hard your GPU is forced to work. The goal? A setup that looks incredible while performance is still silky.

Terrain LOD: The Biggest FPS Killer

The Terrain Level of Detail (LOD) setting determines how far out the sim renders detailed landscapes. This is a resource-intensive setting—crank it up, and distant hills turn into mountains and cities gain definition.

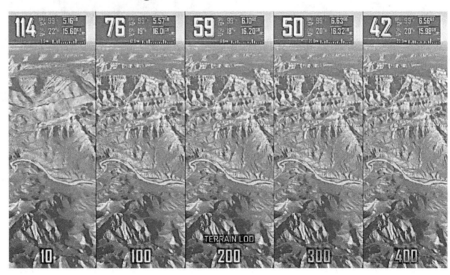

- Going from LOD 10 to 100? Big visual upgrade.
- Beyond LOD 100? Diminishing returns. At LOD 400 (the max setting), the FPS drop is massive, but the difference between 200 and 400 is barely noticeable.

If you're mostly flying at high altitudes or staying in the cockpit, dialing this back can free up performance without a big visual downgrade.

TREES & PLANTS: PRETTY, BUT COSTLY

Vegetation conditions control trees, bushes and overall foliage. They actually have a pretty visible effect on FPS apparently:

Trees: The jump from Medium to High introduces more shadows, but High to Ultra-isn't really visible—although ultra has a more significant performance penalty. High is the place.

Plants: Like Trees this setting uses about 14% more FPS at Ultra for scarcely any extra quality over High.

Terrain Shadows: Where to Draw the Line

Well, Terrain Shadows does not appear to be a big setting, but it affects visuals and FPS tremendously. Settings are OFF, 256, 512, 1024, or 2048.

- OFF to 256? Significant visual improvement.
- More than 256? Almost imperceptible with a bit of severe FPS reduction.

- If you desire quality shadows but don't wish to compromise performance, then 256 is the place to be.

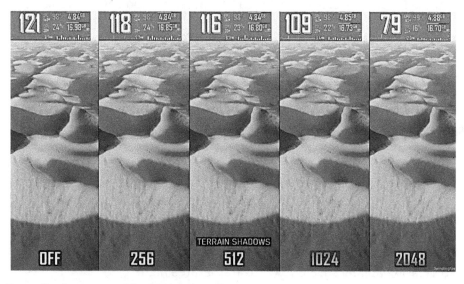

Texture Resolution: No Big FPS Worries

Good news—texture resolution isn't a massive FPS killer. Regardless of whether it's Low, Medium, High, or Ultra, the frame rate disparity is minimal, and if your GPU is VRAM-adequate, Ultra is worth it for crisp cockpit details and uncluttered scenery.

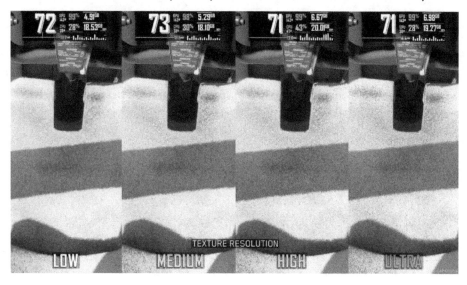

FPS Boosting with DLSS

If you're using NVIDIA's DLSS, updating to the latest version can improve performance. Just replace the old DLSS file in your MSFS folder, and you'll get the best AI-powered upscaling available.

Summing It Up: What's Worth Tweaking?

At the conclusion of the video, Dwindling FPS also presents a table comparing settings from lightest to most resource-intensive. That is truly convenient for customizing your sim:

- Major FPS eaters: Terrain LOD
- Easy wins: Settings like light shafts that boost visuals without hurting performance.

The video concludes with an optimized settings guide—a properly balanced setup that still has a pleasing appearance but keeps framerates high.

MSFS 2024 is a demanding sim, and performance depends on everything from your CPU and GPU to your RAM and SSD. While no single setup works for everyone, having a baseline guide makes tweaking easier. If you're looking for a way to get the best experience, Dwindling FPS's guide is a solid place to start.

Update Your DLSS for better performance

If you are using NVIDIA's DLSS, then make sure you're on the latest version. You can do this by simply overwriting the current old DLSS file in your MSFS folder. This will give you the best AI-upscaling for sharper images and improved performance.

Breaking Down FPS Impact

He includes a very useful table at the end of the video, ranking all the settings from most to least impactful with regards to frame rates, to make fine-tuning your sim easier:

Heavy hitters: Take note that features such as Terrain LOD indeed impose heavy loads on performance, so use them sparingly.

Low-impact adjustments: The rest of the settings, such as light shafts, do not affect frame rates even at maximum when cranked.

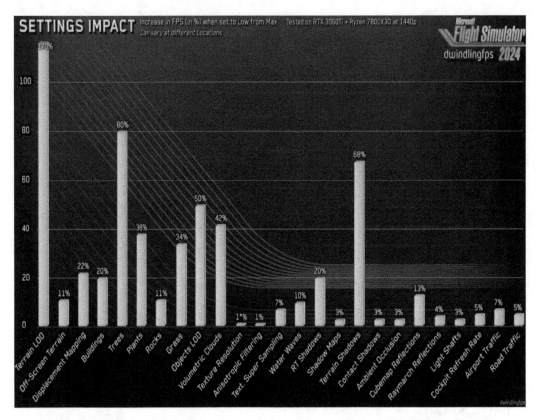

Best Balanced Settings The movie also includes optimized settings-a expertly chosen balance that finds equilibrium between great pictures and smooth performance. Of course, results will vary depending on your gear; MSFS 2024 is a voracious beast, and all the way down to CPU and GPU, RAM and SSD speed, there's an impact. But being well-equipped negates the guesswork.

ENHANCING REALISM WITH VR AND HEAD TRACKING

If you've had a look through our Hardware Guide, then you'll realize the reality that a flight simulator loves his hardware. From Flight controls to GPS units to custom panels, you can literally build a simulated-on-the-fly aircraft cockpit in your house. Everything that's about to change is Virtual Reality turning it around. Instead of merely relying on the physicality of hardware, certain simmers venture into VR setups, which bring their aircraft to life in a complete 3D immersive environment.

Head Tracking: A Step Towards Immersion

Before diving into full-on VR, let's take a look at head tracking - a cheap solution to bring the flight sim experience to the next level. Instead of having to use the hat switch on a joystick to rotate views, head-tracking software will allow one to naturally rotate the head in the direction one wants to rotate, offering more immersive ways of flying without the cost involved in using VR.

Some of the more widely used head tracking options:

- AI Track – Free
- OpenTrack – Free
- SmoothTrack – $10
- Beam Eye Tracker – $30
- TrackHat – $35 - $75
- TrackIR – $150
- Tobii Eye Tracker 5 – $259

AI Track, for example, is an open-source, no-cost tracker available for use with phone cameras or webcams. Installation is somewhat of a hassle, but it's a decent place to start with head tracking.

Virtual Reality: The Next Level

If you want immersion, then VR's for you. A VR headset-a Head-Mounted Display, short for it-is the one that plunges you straight into the cockpit of an airplane and lets you see flight in actual 3D. Add to that motion-tracking controllers, and in VR you can handle the controls as if you were really inside the plane.

A majority of the simmers who do switch say that it's not possible to switch back—VR offers a sense of presence that nothing else does. That being said, it is still evolving technology, and while improving, not all flight simulators presently offer seamless VR integration.

VR Adoption Among Simmers (2024):

- 18% use VR for flight simulation
- 10% own a headset but use it for other games
- 72% do not use VR

Why VR Is So Immersive

Two main conditions determine how realistic an experience in VR will be:

• **Field of View (FOV)** – The bigger the FOV, the more realistic the cockpit will be.

• **Refresh Rate** – More refresh rate gets motion sickness out of the way and smooths performance.

Finally, multi-monitor setups do not feel as real as VR, and the new wraparound monitors require more GPU power and expense.

Challenges with VR in Flight Sim

VR has some disadvantages. High-fidelity airplane models consume a lot of resources and take a hit in VR compared to 2D. The vast majority of pilots wear their VR headset judiciously - removing it for activity such as FMS programming or working on flight plans to then again put it back on while flying takeoffs and landings.

Interaction Methods:

- **Mouse and keyboard** – Workable but sometimes clunky.
- **VR controllers** – Permits hands-on interaction but might not always be convenient.
- **Physical flight controls** – Joystick, yoke, and rudder pedals are the most suitable.

Performance Considerations

Unlike traditional flight sims, VR isn't a simple plug-and-play experience. Even with high-end PCs, achieving smooth performance takes some tweaking. Running a performance test, such as the SteamVR Performance Test, can help determine if your setup is VR-ready. Generally, you'll need:

- A modern PC with Windows 10 or later
- A high-performance CPU and GPU
- At least 16GB of RAM

Choosing a VR Headset for Flight Sim

For a complete VR setup, you'll need:

- A VR-compatible flight simulator (MSFS, X-Plane, DCS World, etc.)
- A VR headset (along with any necessities such as base stations or controllers)

Physical flight controls (optional but suggested for an optimal experience)

Top VR headsets for flight simulation in 2023:

- HP Reverb G2 – 34%
- Oculus Quest 2 – 24%
- Oculus Rift S – 7%
- Meta Quest 3 – 7%

Some headsets, such as Windows Mixed Reality (WMR) headsets, offer more affordable and easier entry points to VR without base stations external to the headset. Others, such as Oculus headsets, require a Facebook account to use.

Enhancing the VR Experience

Since it's so inconvenient to type on a keyboard while in VR, most simmers keep their hardware setup to a minimum. A joystick or yoke with programmable buttons is ideal for easy access to basic controls like landing gear or flaps. Voice control software like VoiceAttack ($10), which converts voice commands to keyboard shortcuts, is another excellent helper.

Motion Sickness in VR

VR motion sickness does exist, especially among the beginners. There are simmers who experience post-flight nausea lasting minutes and even hours after that initial VR flight. The thing is, adaptation is incremental; start with small steps, build the tolerance.

Motion Sickness Among Simmers:

- 49% at least sometimes

// Navigraph FlightSim Community Survey

VR in Different Flight Simulators

Nowadays, every major flight simulator supports VR with MSFS at the forefront of

- Microsoft Flight Simulator (MSFS) – 66%
- X-Plane – 9%
- DCS World – 21%

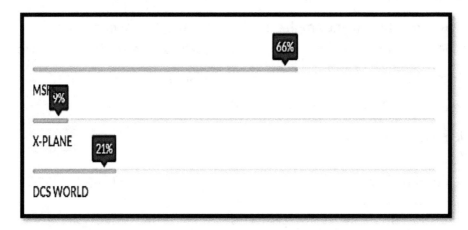

For the best VR experience, many simmers want to have the best frame rate of 45 FPS.

The Future of VR in Flight Simulation

As technology gets better and better, VR is becoming more accessible and smoother. Better hardware, better software support, with prices dropping-nothing stands in the way of VR becoming an outright necessity for the most realistic flight simulation experience available.

CHAPTER 9

CAREER MODE AND CHALLENGES

Microsoft Flight Simulator 2024 features an innovative Career Mode where the players get to engage themselves in the world of flying. Of course, everyone is interested in – what it has to offer, and how does Career Mode make flying experience possible? Let's put it into perspective.

What Is Career Mode in MSFS 2024?

In the older flight simulators, it was the thrill of a pilot's adrenaline that one felt. Now, in this Career Mode, you will be building an aviation career: acquiring certifications, running businesses, and growing a fleet with some of the world's finest aircraft.

It documents your journey from a junior license holder scraping together to an accomplished professional piloting highly specialized aircraft and operating your own flight business. Cargo delivery, VIP charters, or search and rescue, the Career Mode is dynamic and yours alone in every sense of the phrase.

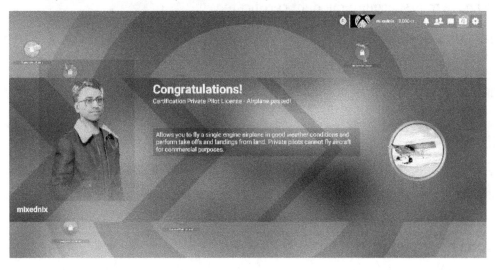

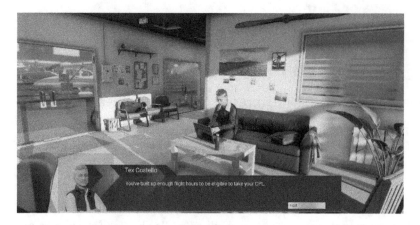

The growth in the Career Mode is founded upon four main bases: Certifications, Specializations, Missions, and Companies.

1. Certifications

There are over 20 certificates that give you access to numerous specializations. These licenses regulate which aircraft you are allowed to pilot and whether or not you are allowed to do it for profit. Should you wish to own a charter service, for example, then you will have to first acquire the right certificate.

2. Specializations

Your Specializations are defined by your certifications, i.e., the type of missions you will be undertaking in the world of aviation. The example is the Search & Rescue license; the associated missions will show up on your map automatically.

3. Missions

Depending on your Specialization, procedurally generated missions of every kind will be accessible all over the world. Missions differ in difficulty, duration, and reward, so some of them will require advanced aircraft or high-level skills.

Missions are divided into two categories:

- **Standard Missions** - regular tasks that reward moderately.
- **Special Missions** - more complex missions that involve some of the planes, longer flights, or harsh conditions, but with high rewards.

4. Companies After you accumulate sufficient Credits, you can establish your own aviation firm. There are even more missions, which grant passive income to it for the rest of your life. However, running a company is not all about collecting cash-you'll also

need to pay for upkeep of the airplanes, follow legislation and regulations, and gain a good reputation in case you wish to go out of business.

Speaking of aircraft maintenance, wear-and-tear is a fact of life in MSFS 2024. You just have to service your aircraft every now and then, or else it will malfunction-or worse.

CAREER MODE'S CURRENCIES

Your advancement in Career Mode is based around three key currencies:

Credits - Earned from completing missions and running businesses. Used for buying new aircraft, paying the wages of crews, and other repairs.

EXP (Experience Points): Gained through completion of missions; smooth flights, efficient landings, and safe operations gain bonuses.

Reputation: You're standing in the aviation world. Good reputation increases access to finer aircraft and increases mission returns.

As stated, Reputation will influence earnings and potentially career advancement, but doesn't appear to have an influence on mission types.

Microsoft Flight Simulator 2024's career mode brings depth, progression, and a whole new layer of realism to the series. From a green rookie pilot to a global aviation conglomerate, this addition provides an entirely new way to play flight simulation. Buckle up.

EXPLORING MISSIONS AND CAREER PROGRESSION

Well, Microsoft Flight Simulator 2024 is finally coming on November 19, 2024, which brought about mixed reactions ranging from enthusiasm to argumentative forum discussions among the flight simulation community. Evidently, the following were waiting for the next one; now, anticipation has grown due to the announced release date.

But not everybody is on board just yet. There are gamers who are concerned that upgrading might be costly for those who spent a fortune on add-ons in the 2020 version, while others continue to hold out hope that Microsoft might offer some discounts or upgrade paths to make the transition a little easier.

Aside from that, one of the hot topics is that MSFS 2024 will be released as a new title and not some sort of update. On the one hand, that allows developers to rebuild the simulator from scratch, using new technologies to their fullest extent; on the other hand, there are more than enough questions about compatibility with the existing content and mods. In any case, the more intricate and feature-rich the simulator gets, the higher the excitement level remains.

Aviation Activity System: New Level of Realism for Aviation

Among the most promising new elements that has been added to Microsoft Flight Simulator 2024 is the addition of its so-called Aviation Activity System, which seeks to introduce more structured aviation missions into the game. Rather than just free-flying from one airport to another, players can now engage in a variety of professional aviation careers.

Microsoft has collaborated with real-world agencies, including fire departments, search and rescue teams, and coast guards, to make these missions as realistic as possible.

Real-World Missions & Activities

Some of the many exciting aviation careers featured in the trailers include:

- **Aerial firefighting**–Flying in smoke-filled skies to bomb forest fires with water.
- **Medical evacuations**: Flying critically wounded patients to hospitals.
- **Cargo transport:** Delivering much-needed supplies to hard-to-reach areas.
- **VIP charters:** Flying high-profile clients in private aircraft.
- **Air racing**: To participate in or engage in a series of adrenaline-pumping, high-speed events.

With the incorporation of real-life scenarios, these missions offer not only thrills but also educate players on the various ways aviation is used on a daily basis.

Key Improvements in Core Simulation & Technology

Microsoft Flight Simulator 2024 is not all about new missions—it's also making key improvements to its physics engine, aerodynamics, and performance optimization.

More Realistic Physics & Aerodynamics

Specifically, the game's new multithreaded physics engine means it can be dramatically more accurate in terms of flight dynamics-airplanes feel and respond even more realistically. Look for improved handling of aircraft, but also more realistic aerodynamic forces and other discrete effects like lift, drag, and turbulence.

Whether it's a small Cessna or a jumbo Boeing 747, each and every airplane will be more realistic in different weather and flight conditions.

Performance Optimization via Cloud Streaming

To optimize the performance of the game, MSFS 2024 will utilize a "thin client" architecture via cloud streaming to offload much of the heavy lifting. In other words, what this really means:

- Faster load times
- Less local storage requirement
- Better performance on different hardware setups

Yet to be seen, this technology could be a godsend for gamers low on space or who have lower systems.

Cross-Platform Release

Microsoft is ensuring that Flight Simulator 2024 reaches a wide audience upon its launch by making it available across various platforms. It will be released on:

- Windows PC
- Xbox Series X|S
- Xbox Game Pass (Console, PC and Cloud)

By making MSFS 2024 a day-one arrival on Xbox Game Pass, Microsoft facilitates an appropriate mainstream way in which game-fans have access to the game, rather than an up-front buy. Similarly, cloud plays support facilitates the point where literally anyone with considerably lower-spec machines is able to enjoy the full completeness of flight experience.

Compatibility & Transition from MSFS 2020

The other important question, probably, could be that of existing players about the state of their add-ons and custom content integrated into MSFS 2020. Well, Microsoft has put it into the open and ensured backward compatibility for most third-party add-ons.

That is, all the aircraft, scenery, enhancements should continue to function, and the custom add-ons will be retained and managed within a community folder dedicated to it.

With that being said, developers and modders will continue to be able to enhance the simulator uninterrupted.

A Seamless Transition with Community Folder Support

Microsoft Flight Simulator 2024 is also designed to ensure that the transition from its 2020 equivalent is as seamless as possible through its support for the community folder. For convenience in management and handling of add-ons, this function will simplify handling of add-ons for players and maintain compatibility of the current mods and custom content with the latest version. In offering this extent of continuity, MSFS 2024 guards not only players' time and money invested in their add-ons but also promotes creativity among flight sim enthusiasts. Developers are secure in knowing their work will continue to be relevant and accessible.

Career Mode: The Virtual Pilot's Dream?

For instance, the MSFS 2024 trailer mentions "living the dream in your aviation career," which started to lead people to believe that some kind of structured career mode will exist. While Microsoft and Asobo Studio have not suggested how that would work, the community is hoping this feature will allow users to have an even more immersive way of living real-world aviation careers.

Climbing the Career Ladder

Of course, there is one highly coveted progression where players could progress from pilot training to more specialized roles such as commercial flying, cargo transport, or even search and rescue.

This would be done by earning certifications-a private pilot license (PPL) or an instrument rating through interactive tutorials and missions. This mode would be possible both for gameplay and learning about aviation complexities through having different career paths with unique challenges and objectives. More Realism with Pilot Avatars and Ground Operations MSFS 2024 could include pilot avatars as well, where players would be able to create and customize their in-game characters. It would add another level of immersion, especially when avatars would be included in the career mode or interactive missions.

On the other hand, the game also seems to be building up on the ground. The trailer shows realistic action in the way of refueling, cargo loading, and passenger boarding, but brings about the question on whether or not players will be able to play as a ground crew. That would definitely create an additional sense of dynamism, one where player could experience aviation beyond the scope of actually flying

Massive overhauls continue to push MSFS 2024 to its limits of realism-from the broad, panoramic vistas down to the tiniest details in urban areas. More accurate terrain and photogrammetry data ensure an even more realistic depiction of the world. Cities, buildings, and landmarks will be more realistic than ever, textured with intricate textures and realistic architecture that brings this virtual world to life.

A More Dynamic World

It's not just a question of prettier landscapes-the world is a more immersive one. Some of the followings are what the game can deliver:

- **Advanced Weather Effects:** More realistic storm systems, auroras, even tornadoes that actually affect flight conditions.
- **Seasonal Changes:** Dynamic environments that change with the seasons, from autumn leaves to snowy winters and spring blooms.
- **Improved Water Physics**: Realistic reflections and interaction with aircraft and boats.
- **Wildlife Activity:** Animal migrations, herding behaviors create a lived-in world.

Community Responses and Anticipations

The flight sim community has reacted to the MSFS 2024 announcement with considerable enthusiasm and cautious optimism. Though most are extremely impressed with the new game's technologies, including enhanced physics, aerodynamics, and interactive environments, some fear that the new game will be too expensive and incompatible with existing content as well.

While the gamers are very positive regarding updates to be released after the launch, it is only expected that Microsoft would keep refining and adding to the foundation based on community feedback. The long-term success will therefore depend on how issues are handled by the developers and how the improvements are continually made.

A New Era for Flight Simulation

Microsoft Flight Simulator 2024 is set to change everything. With new game features, enhanced simulation technology, and stunning environmental updates, it's set to set the bar even higher for flight simulation. Features like the Aviation Activity System—where users can participate in aerial firefighting, medical evacuation, and cargo shipping—go on to add still further to what is achievable within the game.

While there are still many questions, there is no doubt: MSFS 2024 will be in a class of its own when it arrives, November 19, 2024. Whether an experienced old-time flying veteran or completely new to such flying experiences, there could not have been a more promising future for aviation simulations.

LANDING CHALLENGES AND BUSH TRIPS

Maybe not the way most will begin their review of Microsoft Flight Simulator 2024, I didn't spend my first few hours with it in the air, flying. I was on the ground, running around, exploring, and taking a look at some very pretty things about the world from down low. From up high, the game is as pretty as its already stunning 2020 predecessor, but to view it from the ground? That is a whole other level of immersion.

You can descend on the planet anywhere, open the cockpit hatch, and gaze in wonder at the stunning amount of detail: Frosty winter light filtering through thick alpine trees on snowy mountain slopes, endless deserts with bleached rocks scattered over dry flora, and wind-sculpted sea cliffs plunging onto serene pebble beaches with sparkling waters. As long as you don't fly through some of the seedier-looking cityscapes, everything is incredibly realistic. If Flight Simulator 2020 already sold you on the idea of the ultimate travel experience in a box, then 2024 does it one better by making discovery a reason to get in itself.

MICROSOFT FLIGHT SIMULATOR 2024 AT A GLANCE

- Developer: Asobo
- Publisher: Xbox Game Studios
- Platform: Played on PC
- Availability: Available now on Xbox Series X/S, Game Pass, and PC (Steam, Windows)

With that said, Microsoft Flight Simulator 2024 has large shoes to fill.

The 2020 version was already a wonder—the improbably detailed, world-spanning simulation. So, what would possibly make a full-fledged sequel worthwhile? Not so much a total revolutionary overhaul, 2024 takes its predecessor and polishes and builds upon it in intelligent and meaningful ways. Rather than reinventing the wheel, Asobo has refined and built upon what made the last game so breathtaking, marrying its open-ended simulation with new structured experiences. For all the overhauls and retuning, at its core, the magic of Flight Simulator remains intact. This painfully accurate 1:1 simulation of the planet, built from real data, is now even better honed, with more realistic cloud formations, more spectacular weather effects, and more vivid detail in its scenery.

Indeed, describing its 29,401-mile computer recreation of Earth as the greatest open world ever created within a game would not be hyperbole. It is a stunning achievement of craft that provides unlimited freedom and stunning vistas, whether one is soaring above endless expanses of wilderness or weaving through the colorful lights of a bustling city. But to actually put a finger on how much this version has evolved, there is one gob-smacking new feature: at any one point in time, you pull the camera right back-until you are viewing Earth from space. From there, you spin the globe, select another spot, then smoothly zoom in as the terrain shifts before you-mountains, valleys, and forests that pop into view in real-time with altering seasons and burgeoning ecosystems. Breathtaking is not quite the word. But 2024 is not all about better graphics or more complex sightseeing. One of the biggest additions is the Career Mode, which fixes one of the original game's biggest problems: making the experience more accessible. While Flight Simulator 2020 introduced curated challenges and sightseeing tours, at times it felt like there was a humongous chasm between those newbie-friendly activities and the deep, complex mechanics of full simulation. Career Mode is what fills in that gap, combining all of the different elements of the game into some form of cohesive experience. Casual player or hardcore flying aficionado, it gives a real sense of progression that makes Flight Simulator 2024 so much more enjoyable and rewarding an experience. Ultimately, while it might not be a complete reinvention, Microsoft Flight Simulator 2024 still delivers something special. It builds on an already remarkable foundation, refining the experience in ways that make it even more immersive, beautiful, and accessible. Whether you're a seasoned pilot or just someone looking to explore the world from a new perspective, this is an experience worth taking to the skies for.

credited: Asobo/Microsoft/Eurogamer

A MORE STRUCTURED, INTERACTIVE AIR TRAVEL EXPERIENCE

Career Mode in Microsoft Flight Simulator 2024 is the most "game-like" the series has ever been, and with it comes XP progression, mission grading, skill trees, and a linear path to success. Hardcore simulation fans might read this and say it's a deviation from the purist experience, but for the majority of players, including myself, it's an added extra.

At its core, Career Mode makes Flight Simulator into a game of incremental progression: flying tiny planes, doing contract jobs for money and experience, and slowly working your way up to running your own air company over the course of time. Variation of mission keeps things engaging: quick, simple passenger flights give way to more specialized forms of mission like crop-dusting, delivering cargo, and even high-risk helicopter rescues. Since these missions have specific start and finish points, it is simpler to enjoy Flight Simulator during shorter periods of play without having to prepare for extended range flights. What actually makes this system clever, however, is the manner in which it plays out: getting access to new aircraft, mission types and business arrangements isn't about grinding experience, but obtaining specific licences in independent flight genres. You start with aeroplanes and helicopters, but the opportunity to learn more specialist flying will gradually open up. There isn't any getting around doing these licences-you have to attend lessons, then take exams and flight tests that demonstrate you really do know what you're doing.

Essentially, Career Mode is a form of in-flight school, teaching the player everything from the very basics to the more devious aspects of flight. It's a considered learning curve that not only makes the game more enjoyable but also gives the player a good grounding for the rest of the simulator-from smooth as silk landings all the way down to flying through air currents skillfully. Whether you're a casual flyer or an aspiring pilot, this mode adds a new level of depth and accessibility to the experience.

Image credit: Asobo/Microsoft/Eurogamer

A Mixed Bag of Innovation and Weaknesses

While Flight Simulator 2024's Career Mode does offer some form and progression, it isn't without its flaws. The variety between each procedurally generated mission type is very limited, which can make the already slow grind feel stagnant after a while. And then there's the voice acting, or lack thereof. Instead of hiring actual voice actors, Asobo relies on AI-generated voices for the numerous locations worldwide. Unfortunately, this translates to robotic, deadpan readings full of mispronunciations to pull you out of it right away. It's the opposite of how nice the game is, almost defacing a work of art with sloppy brushstrokes. That being said, Career Mode is still a success.

And then, naturally, there's the game's retro-style progression system, which runs through in delightful counterpoint to the otherwise confusing Free Flight sandbox, allowing players to seamlessly switch into the sim, and to learn more about flying. Outside of Career Mode, as well, Flight Simulator 2024 is a rich-content game. Asobo has supplemented the game since its initial release with a plethora of handpicked challenges and contained excursions, offering hundreds of one-off events. There's rally racing, low-altitude flying, landing challenges and sightseeing discovery flights-many of which feature weekly leaderboards for added competitive flavor. Another key new feature is the World Photography Mode, putting that new camera rig through its paces in style. This mode, basically, turns aviation into a work of art: challenging the player to capture breathtaking vistas of mega buildings, national parks, ancient geoglyphs, European castles, and even wildlife-all from accurate angles.

Whether you're soaring in a hot air balloon, flying over the clouds, or even on foot, these photography challenges add a fresh twist to the experience. I mean, yes, it's still all about flight, certainly. But these meticulously crafted experiences against some of the world's most beautiful landscapes looking at their very best prove that Flight Simulator 2024 is, in fact far more than just a technological marvel, but a celebration of the pure majesty of flight.

Image credit: Asobo/Microsoft/Eurogamer

Targeting High, But Not Without Turbulence

It's hard not to be impressed at the sheer ambition of Flight Simulator 2024. Asobo has expanded on its 2020 title in style, crafting something that feels even more immersive and substantial. Some of the most important improvements are in its back-end tech. A new streaming system—assuming your internet can handle it—substantially reduces hard-drive space requirements by streaming in hand-crafted landmarks, improved terrain data, and aircraft in real-time, without requiring enormous downloads.

That said, the game at times feels like it's straining under its own ambitions. PC performance is uneven, even accounting for the increased system demands, and the redesigned controller layout is so Byzantine that even someone with extra fingers would find it difficult to get the hang of. But despite the growing pains, Flight Simulator 2024 is an ambitious, thoughtful experience.

But its launch was anything but smooth. That is, it was a mess. Even though Asobo has continued to make significant improvements since, the game still feels like it was rushed out the door—a familiar issue with some of Microsoft's big first-party launches. Sometimes that incomplete feel is fairly overt: Parts of Career Mode's progression tree and some of the challenge activities are still marked "coming soon." Even the in-game store has been locked off nearly three weeks after launch, which means players who previously bought planes or compatible DLC from the 2020 version still can't access them. For all its ambition and innovation, Flight Simulator 2024 still has some turbulence to ride out.

A Rocky Liftoff, but a Promising Flight

There are more than enough indications that Flight Simulator 2024 wasn't ready for takeoff. Most glaringly, the Bush Trips-those enchanted guided tours across interesting terrain-have been missing since 2020. The most anyone can hope for is nebulous mention of them coming back in some future patch. And then there are the bugs, and lots of them. I have flown flights wherein my chocks seemed to glue themselves to the wheels, preventing me from ever taking off. Passengers complain of flying too high or of flying too fast, even though in-game UI says all's well. The landmarks sometimes just refuse to load, and at least once my controls stopped responding mid-flight to send me into a spiral into the ground. If that's frustrating for casual fliers, I can only imagine what the horror hardcore simmers have to go through with more advanced aircraft systems. There is still lag to be noted as well, and that's concerning considering how much Flight Simulator 2024 depends on Microsoft servers. That being said, all these launch mishaps don't feel like they're irreparable. Asobo has a great track record for post-launch support, and they've already been reasonably quick to listen to community feedback. And when everything's humming along smoothly—good show, most of the time—the game is absolutely stunning.

Impressive scale, depth, and beauty for this sequel. It is arguably not as innovative as its ancestor, but it refines and expands the experience so that it is more welcoming and appealing. Flight Simulator 2024 is maybe not a new benchmark, but it remains a stunning salute to love of flight and discovery.

CHAPTER 10

TIPS AND TRICKS FOR THE BEST FLIGHT EXPERIENCE

1. It's More Than Just a Game

Microsoft Flight Simulator 2024 is not a game but a flight simulation experience which is incredibly detailed and as realistic as possible. The moment you grab the controller, it's as if you are preparing for an actual flight.

2. Customize Your Controls for an Enhanced Experience

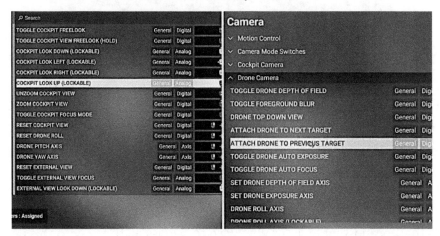

It's a good idea before you start playing to have your control settings sorted out. Whether playing with the keyboard and mouse, an Xbox controller, or a flight stick, having your controls perfectly tuned is what can really make a difference.

One of the more significant adjustments is sensitivity. It is trying to simulate a flight experience as realistic as possible; therefore, settings like pitch and roll need to find balance with your capacity to be comfortable. Also, inspect your keys bindings- sometimes the default works just fine, but a bit of tweaking will make them much more intuitive.

3. Enable the Assistance Features in an effort to enhance flying.

If you are a beginner with MSFS 2024 or like more comfort while getting accustomed to the controls, you can activate in-game assistance settings at your own will. There are two main presets:

- **All Assists** – for beginners, this option provides maximum assistance in flight.
- **Default Assists** – standard features of assistance, better for advanced players.
- Seek out Customization in your options, depending upon what experience you feel might work best for your particular skill set.

4. Begin with the Tutorial Before You Fly

The truth is that for most individuals who wish to bypass all the way to this new game mode right away, a major course on general aviation begins with just tutorials. They fill you up with your various techniques you would experience with later, perhaps challenging flights.

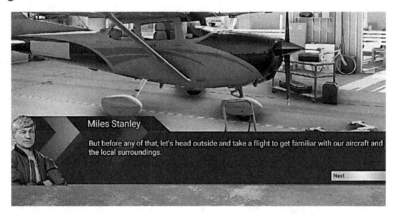

Even Career Mode can serve as a helpful guide, offering structured missions that gradually increase in difficulty.

5. Explore Career Mode Early

One of the biggest expansions in MSFS 2024 is Career Mode, which introduces new aircraft and mission types. You're not limited to just planes and helicopters—you can even fly hot air balloons!

Career Mode allows you to get a job of different types, which are:

- **charter pilot:** Flying commercial or private plane and carrying passengers.
- **rescue pilot:** Performing rescue missions by flying.

Since there are different careers, you can have multiple save profiles and experience flying of different times.

6. Step Out and Explore on Foot

Although flying forms the bulk of MSFS 2024, you are not locked in a cockpit at all times. Some of the missions involve walking around, whether this involves cruising around a commercial airplane cabin or taking some breathtaking views from some isolated mountain landing site.

This feature transforms MSFS 2024 into more than just a flight simulator; it's a discovery experience, as well, where you can indulge the luxury of slowing down and taking in the enormous amount of detail the game was constructed with.

7. Tweak Your Graphics Settings for Optimal Vision

While breathtaking visuals are worth the system strain. Dialing in the graphics settings allows you to balance performance vs. realism.

- Begin with medium if in doubt.
- Reduce if there is a sense of lag.
- If there is an incredibly powerful machine, then go on and switch max settings on.

Your objective should always be to obtain as smooth frames as can be obtained. Until you reach it, fiddle with any setting in or out until such optimal setting appears to emerge.

By following these steps, you'll be set up for an even more enjoyable and immersive experience in Microsoft Flight Simulator 2024. Whether touring the world, mastering the many various planes, or simply gazing about at the views, this sim offers a lot to do, look at, discover, and enjoy.

PERFORMANCE OPTIMIZATION FOR SMOOTH GAMEPLAY

Microsoft Flight Simulator 2024 has finally arrived on Xbox Series X/S and PC. While the launch did hit a couple of bumps in the server, the game itself is truly breathtaking. Asobo Studio has done it again to bring the incredibly detailed world with aircraft made almost perfect. This is truly the flight sim of one's dreams—but to beginners, it is entirely and utterly overwhelming.

But diving into them with all of that to master will be daunting-even with the game-on-Game Pass. And most often, it won't be a problem. There are numerous methods of acclimatizing to the experience. If you're a beginner or returning after an extended break, these ten tips are essential to get you in style:

1. Take Your Time

If you've played the previous versions, you already know already-patience is necessary. There's so much to learn, don't rush. Every aircraft has a different flying style, and with different parameters like un-predictable weather, unique runways, and mission objectives, take your time to practice.

2. Start with Tutorials

Yes, you can go into Free Flight mode and take off from anywhere on the planet. But if you're a newbie, that's not a good idea. Do the tutorials first. They'll get you through the absolute basics, such as taking off and landing and maneuvering your aircraft. Get those down pat before advancing to the more complex mechanics.

3. Customize Your Controls

Microsoft Flight Simulator 2024 enables you to completely tailor your controls, whether that is mouse and keyboard, controller, or flight stick. Once you have become accustomed to the basics, make sure that you tune the controls so that they feel more individual to you and are smoother, more intuitive to use.

4. Use Assistances

The game does contain a lot of aid features that can be enabled to make things easier. Go into settings and enable the following: Auto-Rudder, Assisted Yoke, and Controller Sensitivity adjustments. You can also enable markers for waypoints, flight routes, and even taxi ribbons. If you like it super forgiving, you can even disable aircraft stress, engine failure, and fuel constraints.

5. Stay in the Cockpit View

Even though there are different camera views available to utilize, the cockpit view is more followed by a beginner. It offers you a higher sense and consciousness of aircraft handling since you are also able to appreciate the detailed instrument panels. If you are looking for panoramic views, use World Photographer Mode instead of making use of outside cameras while in flight.

6. Tweak Your Settings

Aside from assists and controls, there are literally hundreds of options you can tweak, from focus to zoom and intelligent camera modes. You'll also have the option to adjust cockpit camera height, free-look speed, and instrument presentation. You'll also be able to play with the flight realism settings, disabling some of the interface elements to clean things up. Try it out and see what works for you.

7. Explore Career Mode & Specializations

Aside from these tutorials, Career Mode is also a relatively tidy means of improving your skills. You choose your starting location where you begin and will end up earning your Private Pilot License, and receive the rest of the licenses as you transition into the other specialties.

Level 8 unlocks Skydive Aviation, which presents more challenging missions. You also have the opportunity to train in rotorcraft licenses and conduct special missions such as Search and Rescue or Aerial Construction. Search for the Aviator Performance tab, available post-missions, for areas to improve.

8. Monitor Mission Difficulty Ratings

Some missions in Career Mode are harder than others, so don't forget to consider their star ratings as well. Everyone has a degree of difficulty that is assigned to it. The ones with bigger challenges may have bad weather or complicated flights. If your intention is for enjoyment and not something formal, play the simplest to advance smoothly.

9. Optimize Graphics for Performance

Microsoft Flight Simulator 2024 is a resource-intensive game, and you can actually do something about that by adjusting some of the settings to your liking. You can fiddle with terrain and object detail, texture resolution, cloud quality, and even windshield effects. So, try until you reach that sweet spot between performance and aesthetics—the type where you don't have everything cranked up to Ultra.

	Min Spec	Recommended Spec	Ideal Spec
MIN OS VERSION	Windows 10 *With Latest Update*	Windows 10 *With Latest Update*	Windows 10 *With Latest Update*
DIRECT X VERSION	DX12	DX12	DX12
CPU	AMD Ryzen 2600X *or* Intel Core i7-6800K	AMD Ryzen 7 2700X *or* Intel Core i7-10700K	AMD Ryzen 9 7900X *or* Intel it-14700K
GPU	Radeon RX 5700 *or* GeForce GTX 970	Radeon RX 5700 XT *or* GeForce RTX 2080	Radeon RX 7900 XT *or* GeForce RTX 4080
VRAM	4 GB	8 GB	12 GB
RAM	16 GB	32 GB	64 GB
STORAGE	50 GB	50 GB	50 GB

10. Buy a Flight Stick

You can do it with a standard controller or keyboard and mouse, but a flight stick does make a difference. There are solutions for advanced flight controls - like the T. Flight Hotas One for $99.99 with 14 buttons along with a precision joystick, or the reasonably good Turtle Beach Velocity One Flight stick for $129.99, with 27 programmable buttons supported by a customizable settings app companion. If the flight-simming is serious, high-grade flight sticks would be an option.

Ready for Takeoff?

Microsoft Flight Simulator 2024 is a phenomenal experience, but one that pays huge dividends in terms of patience and practice. Take your time, play with assistances where necessary, and adjust the settings to suit your style of gameplay. Above all, have fun with it-there's an entire world up there to witness from the skies. Happy flying!

HIDDEN SHORTCUTS AND PRO-LEVEL SETTINGS

Categories:

☐ Autopilot ☐ Banner Hook ☐ Banner Pole ☐ Brakes ☐ Camera

☐ Camera (Cockpit) ☐ Camera (Drone) ☐ Camera (External) ☐ Camera (Photo Mode)

☐ Camera (Slew) ☐ Communications ☐ Developer Mode ☐ Firefighting

☐ Flight Control Surfaces ☐ Instruments ☐ Landing Gear ☐ Lights ☐ Miscellaneous

☐ Player Character ☐ Power Management ☐ Skydive System ☐ Tools ☐ VR

Action	Keyboard Command	Category
Toggle Active Pause	P	Tools
Toggle Pause	ESC	Tools
Set Pause Off	ESC	Tools
Toggle EFB	TAB	Tools
Toggle Pushback	ALT + P	Tools
Back to Fly	ALT + SPACE	Tools
Sim Rate	ALT + R	Tools
Toggle CFD	ALT + 5	Tools
Toggle Landing Ribbon	ALT + 4	Tools
Toggle Nameplates	ALT + 2	Tools

General Tools:

- **Flight Assistant:** Switch Flight Assistant on/off with `ALT + 1`.
- **New UI Window Mode**: Switch on using `RIGHT ALT`.
- **Screen Narrator**: Switch on/off with `ALT + Backspace`.
- **Skip RTC**: Press `ESC` directly.
- **Headphone Simulation**: Press `ALT + H` to switch on/off.
- **Next Flight Phase:** Go ahead with `ALT + N`.
- **Back on Track**: To switch back on course, press `SHIFT + B`.

VR Controls:

- Reset VR Camera: `SHIFT`.
- toggle VR Mode on/off: `CTRL + TAB`.
- toggle VR Toolbar: `ALT + T`.

Camera Controls:

- Change SmartCam Targets: Next with `SHIFT + Y`, previous with `SHIFT + R`.
- Turn Smart Camera on/off: Press `CTRL + B`.
- Cockpit & External Views: Reset with `BACKSPACE`, or set angles with `SHIFT` + direction keys.

Engine & Power Management:

- **Start & Stop Engine**: Automatic start with `CTRL + E`, stop with `CTRL + SHIFT + E`.
- **Throttle Adjustments:** Throttle increase (R), throttle decrease (F) or detent switch using CTRL + R, CTRL + F.
- **Mixture & Propeller Control**: Mixture change using H and Y or propeller pitch using G and T.

Instruments & Navigation:

- Set Altimeter: ` `.
- Navigation Settings: NAV1 `CTRL + D`, VOR OBS `CTRL + 0` and ADF `CTRL + 9`.
- Autopilot Controls: Activate supergnat autopilot (`CTRL + 1`), activate altitude hold (`CTRL + F2`), etc.

Flight & Gear:

- Landing Gear Toggle: `/`.
- Flaps: Extend (`B`), retract (`V`), or raise/retract with `CTRL + B/V`.
- Rudder & Ailerons Control: Rudder left (`Q`), right (`E`), aileron trim (`J`/`L`).

Brakes & Emergency:

- Brakes Apply: Just press `SPACE`.
- Toggle Parking Brakes: Press `CTRL + SPACE`.
- Left & Right Brakes: `NUM /` for the left, `NUM ` for the right.

Autopilot:

- Engage Specific Holds: NAV1 (`CTRL + F7`), heading hold (`CTRL + F5`), or altitude hold (`CTRL + F2`).
- Adjust Reference Values: Use `CTRL + INSERT/DELETE` for speed, `CTRL + PAGE UP/DOWN` for altitude.

Communication & ATC:

- Open ATC Panel: Hit `\\`.
- Quick Reply: Just hit `ENTER`.
- Select ATC Options: Use number keys (`0-9`).

Special Functions:

- Switch Water Rudder On / Off: `CTRL + /`.
- Switch Master Battery & Alternator On / Off: `CTRL + Z`.
- Flashlight On / Off: `ALT + F`.
- Firefighting Controls: Spray (`Z`), operate scoops/doors (`Z`).

Learning and mastering resources for flight simulation

If you're ready to start learning to fly using a flight simulator, you've come to the right location! This tutorial has everything, from virtual flight school add-ons to online flight training.

No matter whether you use free materials or spend money on professional courses, well will lead you through your options, such as how a simulator can ready you for real flight school.

Learning to Fly on YouTube (Free)

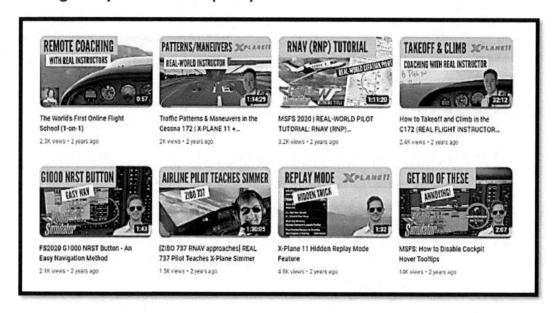

Next best place to learn flight simulation on YouTube: Totally free, with tutorials on close enough any aviation topic. As there is already loads of great instructive content, the top channels will be the following:

For Airliner Enthusiasts

AviationPro: Run by real Boeing 777 & 787 pilot, with airliner flying coverage and VATSIM.

flightdeck2sim – Boeing 737 Captain and Type Rating Instructor offering detailed tutorials.

320 Sim Pilot – Airbus A320 pilot teaching you how to fly the plane realistically.

For General Aviation Pilots

If you're interested in smaller planes, PilotEdge has excellent training content on airspace, ATC communication, and general aviation operations. Their workshop and training rating video playlists are a must-watch.

For Real-World Flight Students

While these channels are meant for real pilots, they are helpful lessons for simulator users who want to fly as realistically as possible:

- Angle of Attack
- Boldmethod
- MzeroA Flight Training

Also, do check out our Flight Sim Coach channel where we combine flight sim tips with instructor led lessons of real students.

Downside of YouTube? The videos are free but are more about acquiring views than having learning arranged in an orderly manner. And worst of all, you get no feedback on your flying whatsoever.

Online Flight Lessons, Personalised ($70 - $80 /hr)

Think of having a qualified, licensed flight instructor guiding you through your simulator session in real time. That's what we do!

How It Works

- Log in through Zoom and share your screen so that your instructor can see your cockpit.
- Get instant feedback, customized exercises, and graphical explanations.
- Our exclusive FSC Link software enables your instructor to see your flight data, trigger failures, even change the weather to make training even more realistic.

Why Choose Live Instruction?

Steer clear of any bad habits that a software lesson simply won't catch.

- Be taught by instructors who are current with aviation regulations, safety, and testing requirements.
- Be taught actual application of flight software like ForeFlight.
- Be taught by an instructor who is a specialist in your aircraft type and flight goals.
- Whether you are a real pilot in training or a flight sim enthusiast, personalized instruction can take your skills to the next level.

Built-in Flight Lessons (Free) – Microsoft Flight Simulator

If you prefer to learn on your own, MSFS has in-game tutorials for the following:

✔ Basic controls & cameras

✔ Attitudes & instruments

✔ Takeoff & landing

✔ Traffic patterns & navigation

✔ First solo flight

These lessons utilize the Cessna 152, simple and uncomplicated flying training aircraft. The training is conducted at the Sedona Airport (KSEZ), pictorial but, still, challenging airport because of the high altitude on which it is located.

Limitation of Built-In Lessons

While the online instructor is good and provides some great tips, there are a few disadvantages: Instructions are basic and don't react dynamically to your responses. Scarcely any use of visual aids, which can make it more difficult to learn for visually-oriented learners. Covers the "what" but not necessarily the "how" or "why" of crucial flight principles.

MSFS lessons are adequate as a starting point, but more complex procedures, not to mention other aircraft, do require more training.

Ready to Take Off?

From YouTube tutorials to official lessons on the internet, there are more than enough options out there to advance your flight simming abilities. From casual in-sim flying to serious flight school preparation, the resources you're seeking are available.

X-PLANE

In-game flight school with progressive lessons is included in X-Plane 12. Text-based instructions with simple graphics lead you through the different ways of flying-never confusing. For example, if it wants to teach turning, then the elevator controls are automatically disabled so that a skill is learned at a time.

The keyboard commands are introduced gradually in the lessons to get you accustomed to the controls.

Lessons are divided into three broad categories:

- **General Aviation:** Takeoffs, landings, traffic patterns, and taildragger takeoffs with aircraft such as the SR-22, C172, and Stinson L5.
- **Navigation**: VOR navigation and ILS approaches.
- **Helicopter:** Helicopter basic operations on the Sikorsky S-76C.

X-Plane also has visualization tools to assist with difficult topics like VOR radials. When the instructions are text-only and not very long, very visual learners will have difficulty.

Some lessons include report cards with numeric grades to track your progress.

Even the phone version of X-Plane includes a flight school, providing you with an inexpensive means to practice basic flight on your tablet or phone.

Prepar3D

Prepar3D lacks in-game flying lessons, but you can keep learning with third-party products like remote training or the FSFlyingSchool add-on.

FSX (Microsoft Flight Simulator X)

FSX also includes in-flight flight lessons from popular flight school instructor Rod Machado. His engaging and humorous teaching has launched many real pilots into the air. If you have FSX, it's definitely worth trying a lesson from Rod!

FLIGHT SIM TRAINING ADD-ONS

For those who want a more formal learning process, several add-ons expand the stock training capabilities within X-Plane and MSFS:

FSFlyingSchool ($44.95): A flight instructor add-on for MSFS, X-Plane, FSX, and P3D. It provides voice-guided lessons, evaluation, flight challenges, and can handle multiple aircraft-from a small aircraft to airliners. There is a free demo.

TakeFlight Interactive ($89): This add-on is designed for private pilot training. It has a virtual instructor, scoring capability, and leaderboard. Works on MSFS, X-Plane 11/12, Prepar3D v4/5 (with the A2A Simulations C172), and FSX. Comes with a free trial lesson.

MSFS-Specific Training Add-Ons

FS Academy ($20-30 per pack): A set of mission packs for VFR, IFR, nav, Airliner training (A320), and emergency scenarios such as "Miracle on the Hudson." It does include some PDF ground school content. Note that these packs are not currently compatible with FS2024.

X-Plane Specific Training Add-Ons

Gleim X-Plane Flight Training Course (XFTC) ($99.95): Private pilot flight training employing an FAA-sanctioned syllabus with video lessons, checkpoints, and instructions utilizing software. Not including MSFS or IFR training. Offered in demo form free.

Sporty's X-Plane 12 VFR Scenarios (Free or $9.95): Provides training scenarios for procedures such as steep turns, S-turns and ILS approaches. The paid version has a higher number of private pilot exercises. The software also prevents aircraft from responding erratically when a paused scenario is continued.

Volunteer Training Organizations (Free)

Virtual Airline Training: Those online clubs which actually experience real simulated airline flight, even formalized training. Example: Boeing 737 training for Southwest Virtual Airlines is on VATSIM.

Online ATC Networks: VATSIM and IVAO are networks that offer radio communications and ATC procedure training. Other clubs like The Pilot Club Flight School and WINGS Over New England provide additional resources.

While these organizations usually provide good free training, their instructors are usually aviation enthusiasts and not certified flight instructors.

FREQUENTLY ASKED QUESTIONS

Can you learn to fly using Microsoft Flight Simulator or X-Plane?

While flight simulators are excellent learning aids, they do not replace flying. You cannot use simulator hours towards your license except in a certified training device. Simulators are great to learn procedures, practice navigation, radio communications, and system management.

Using a simulator for private pilot (PPL) training

Not too long ago, there were teachers who would discourage the home simulators. But since technology has improved, so has their use. Simulators are excellent for procedure practice but can't reproduce the "feel" of flight, especially when landing and installation situations. A VR headset can have a profound impact on immersion for visual flight training.

Using a simulator for instrument training (IR)

Simulators are terrific for IFR training and enable you to practice procedures and remain ahead of the aircraft. However, there are some limitations in their use:

- **Muscle memory:** Without hardware controls, flying does not feel like actual flying.
- **Disorientation:** Actual IMC flying offers chances of spatial disorientation, which a simulator cannot provide.
- **Circling maneuvers:** These are difficult to replicate without VR or head tracking because in a normal monitor setup your perception is not great.

Despite the above limitations, simulators have the ability to save time as well as cost by allowing you to practice problematic IFR flight in the confines of your house.

Do commercial pilots use Microsoft Flight Simulator and X-Plane?

Yes, and the majority of pilots have used simulators to remain proficient, especially when they could not fly an airplane. Some commercial pilots have started their career with simulators as a hobby.

Are there books on flight simulator training?

Yes, there are! Here are a few highly recommended books:

- Microsoft Flight Simulator X for Pilots: Real World Training
- Microsoft Flight Simulator as a Training Aid: A Guide for Pilots, Instructors, and Virtual Aviators

Are online tutorials for flight simulator training available?

Yes, there are! Online platforms such as Udemy and Skillshare offer courses such as:

- Flight Simulator Pilot Course
- Forder Learn to Fly

How do I learn aviation theory?

If you prefer more structure, there are great online ground schools. These courses get you deeply into aviation theory and prepare you for success in real training.

Whether you are a novice or aspire to be a pilot, flight simulators are a fun and affordable way to practice your flying. With the right tools and add-ons, you can take your virtual flight experience to the next level!

INDEX